RESOLVING CONFLICT
AT WORK

RESOLVING CONFLICTS AT WORK

*A guide to negotiation and joint
problem-solving in the workplace*

Steve Hodder

First published in 2012 by Management Books 2000 Ltd
Forge House, Limes Road
Kemble, Cirencester
Gloucestershire, GL7 6AD, UK
Tel: 0044 (0) 1285 771441
Fax: 0044 (0) 1285 771055
Email: info@mb2000.com
Web: www.mb2000.com

British Library Cataloguing in Publication Data is available

ISBN 9781852526801

CONTENTS

FOREWORD

by John Taylor
chief executive of ACAS

This practical 'how to' book is a timely reminder of how far we have come in resolving conflict at work. In the 1970s, when Acas was first established, the employment relations landscape was seen, rightly or wrongly, as far more adversarial than it is today. The media coverage focused very much on the large scale disputes between unions and employers. Many of these disputes were settled around the negotiating table in a certain amount of secrecy.

Fast-forward thirty years and the typical employer has a much wider choice of techniques at his or her disposal for resolving conflict. The growth in the use of mediation, for example, has greatly increased our understanding of how to manage individual and group conflict at work and in society more generally. More pro-active and imaginative ways of preventing conflict have evolved – Acas has, for example, developed its own 'pre-conciliation' service that aims to resolve potential individual disputes before a formal application is made to an employment tribunal.

With such a wide array of alternative dispute resolution procedures does the modern-day manager need to be able to negotiate? The simple answer is 'yes'.

Negotiation is something we all do at work, and in life, all the time. It is a skill that, practised well, has great relevance today and should not be tainted by any negative images we may have of union-management relations in the past. Negotiation, as Steve Hodder argues, is not only very applicable to modern-day conflict but is also a very transferable skill. Negotiation can teach us to appreciate the other person's point of view, to think carefully about how we communicate with each other, how we present our arguments, and how we are able to handle our own and other people's aggression and emotions.

We may be proud of many aspects of the employment relations heritage in this country – for example, the way we have worked to promote fairness and diversity in the workplace – but the passing of time is no guarantee in itself that things will automatically get better. There are always lessons to be learnt from the past and this book rightly uncovers some of the secrets of what should no longer be considered an 'old-fashioned game'.

1

INTRODUCTION

This is a 'how to' book: how to negotiate, how to problem-solve, how to mediate and how to facilitate. In short, this book explores different ways of resolving conflict in the workplace.

Conflict **will** happen at work. It may simply be a clash of personalities. It can be deep-rooted, centring on disagreements over values, expectations which are not being met or on some perceived inequity in treatment. It may result from the behaviour of managers or other employees, from the stress caused by excessive workloads, or from frustration with company procedures. Conflict can also be influenced by external factors, such as problems at home or health issues. It can even just be the consequence of a misunderstanding caused by poor communication. Sometimes it can be a mixture of different factors or have become so deep-seated in the minds of those involved that its original causes are impossible to determine.

What is often not recognised is that conflict in organisations arises as a result of change. The effects of alterations to the status quo will be felt by individuals differently depending on where they are in the hierarchy and what groups they are part of. For some, change will be viewed as a threat, whereas others may see it as an opportunity to be exploited. But, because change at work is inevitable, conflict is both normal and inescapable. What is more, its consequences can be damaging and costly.

The negative effects of conflict in the workplace can be felt in an increased incidence of employment disputes. In non-unionised organisations it can also take the form of more individual grievances, sickness absence, labour turnover, and employment tribunal claims.

Less tangible but nevertheless significant, unresolved conflict at work will lower the morale, commitment and general well-being of employees.

Conflict can take the form of individual disputes (for example, between a manager and a team member), or collective disputes (for example, where a union is recognised, between employee representatives and managers).

But, conflict can also be positive and healthy for an organisation. Conflict can raise issues that need tackling and, far from being destructive, by generating new ideas and fresh ways of working, can benefit the organisation. By resolving conflict, organisations can build co-operation and enhance employee engagement. The key, then, is how the conflict is managed, because this determines its impact.

Over the next few chapters we will be looking at negotiation, mediation, facilitation and joint problem-solving as ways of resolving conflict. The first few chapters of this book focus on resolving collective disputes, but all of the skills and techniques identified are readily transferable for use in tackling individual issues in non-unionised workplaces.

We will start with negotiating. Everyone negotiates. We negotiate at work; we negotiate with our bosses, with our staff and with our work colleagues. We negotiate at home; we negotiate with our friends, with our partners and with our children (in fact children can be very good negotiators, as I know to my cost!). Negotiation is thus a natural, normal social activity. Whenever we want to influence how other people behave, get them to do things our way or resolve disagreements, we engage with them to persuade and offer inducements; sometimes we threaten, and sometimes we compromise. In other words, we negotiate. But, just because we all do it doesn't mean we all do it well.

Many of the skills and techniques of negotiating described here are readily applicable to a range of situations. They can, for example, be used in running a business, in sales and in managing staff. This book, however, deals with negotiating in the workplace. Often this takes the form of collective bargaining, which is generally defined as negotiation between employee representatives and employers to determine terms and conditions of employment on such matters as pay, hours of work, rules and working conditions. But collective bargaining is more than this; it is about how managers and employee representatives get together to manage change, resolve disagreements and solve problems in the workplace. They may not necessarily sit opposite each other across the bargaining table, but they still negotiate.

One of the themes of this book is that negotiation is about conflict management and, as such, can be done well or badly. I spent over thirty years at Acas, conciliating in innumerable disagreements, ranging from individuals making complaints to employment tribunals to major national disputes between employers and trade unions. In doing so, I had the rare and privileged opportunity to watch many excellent negotiators on both sides of the negotiating table in action. I have sought to pull together some of these positive experiences, as well as reflecting on the mistakes I have seen made, and on some I have made myself.

Sometimes derided as a "ritual dance", union–management relations are often criticised for being out of date and dysfunctional. Collective bargaining gets a bad press, influenced no doubt by negative images of 1970s industrial relations. Indeed, negotiating with trade unions has become something of a 'minority pursuit', rarely given much attention by Human Resource professionals.

Despite this, in many workplaces collective bargaining remains the established way in which the competing aspirations of employers and employee representatives can be resolved. Collective bargaining may be a ritual dance, but rituals allow participants to know what to expect. In short, they can help the process of conflict resolution.

The negotiating table is not the only institution to have a bilateral format, together with its own language and seemingly arcane practices. In the House of Commons the Members of Parliament forming the government of the day sit facing their opposite numbers in the Opposition. Between them are two parallel red lines which, traditionally, are two sword-lengths apart. In unionised workplaces lines are drawn in a similar way, with management and trade unions teams lined up on opposite sides of the negotiating table. The adversarial approach to dispute resolution has stood the test of time because, ultimately, it works.

So, is it possible to change the rules of the game? Is it possible for individuals with differing interests to, metaphorically and actually, sit alongside each other and solve problems jointly? A feature of employee relations in the last 20 years has been the development of alternative dispute resolution (ADR) and Win-Win Bargaining. We will look at these techniques in some detail and suggest when they might, and might not, be most appropriate. For now, let me simply make the point that their impact in the workplace, although much discussed, can be exaggerated. Collective bargaining remains the dominant means of determining terms and conditions and resolving disagreements in the unionised workplaces of the UK.

Why is this? Perhaps it is simply because, when push comes to shove, both management and employee representatives feel more comfortable with adversarial bargaining. Both sides have their constituents, those they represent, looking over their shoulders. Negotiators not only have to succeed on their behalf, but have to be seen to succeed. So, when the pressure is on, it feels safer to stay on your own side of the table.

But, does anyone really negotiate anymore? With a long-term decline in trade union membership and influence, and the ending of national bargaining in most industries, you might be forgiven for thinking that collective bargaining no longer matters. Newspapers no longer have industrial relations correspondents; indeed the very term 'industrial relations' is now rarely used. The rise of Human Resource Management, with its emphasis on individualism in the workplace, has demoted industrial relations as a specialism to the sidelines.

All of this has prompted some commentators to talk about the end of 'joint regulation' of terms and conditions of employment by employers and unions. It is certainly true that the most common form of pay determination is by management taking unilateral action. The Workplace Employment Relations Survey (WERS) in 2004 (the latest figures available) found that 70% of workplaces had the pay set for at least some of the employees in this manner. However, this same survey also found that, when the figures were analysed by size of workplace, almost two-thirds of larger workplaces (those with 500 employees or more) set pay for some employees through collective bargaining.

Furthermore, in the public sector, collective bargaining continued to dominate, setting pay in 83% of public sector workplaces. *"Pay determination through collective bargaining has declined since the 1998 survey, but the rate of decline has slowed considerably...and there has even been an increase in bargaining coverage in the public sector"* (WERS 2004).

So, unfashionable though it may be, collective bargaining continues to regulate pay and conditions for many thousands of employees, particularly in large companies and in the public sector. As WERS 2004 found, here at least, the trade union presence has remained stable in recent years.

It is not then the purpose of this book to argue for or against other forms of dispute resolution or employee involvement. Indeed, as we shall see, many of the skills and techniques are 'best practice' in both the traditional and the alternative approaches. What I will be suggesting is that, if we dismiss as outdated everything but a collaborative approach to employee relations, we risk throwing the 'baby out with the bath water'. Despite its decline, traditional collective bargaining remains an important and durable feature of the employment relations scene, so perhaps how we do it currently, and how we could do it better, deserves more of our attention.

New generations of managers have now come into the HR profession, been recruited and trained, who have never dealt with trade unions. Many of these will no doubt spend their careers in those parts of the private sector where trade unionism is largely invisible. But even here, managers may have to deal with trade union officials.

The Employment Relations Act 1999 gave workers attending a disciplinary or grievance hearing the legal entitlement to be accompanied by a work colleague or union official. Workers may ask an official from any trade union to accompany them at a disciplinary or grievance hearing, regardless of whether or not the union is recognised by the employer. Under the legislation, the employer must allow the union official (or work colleague) to address the hearing to put the worker's case, sum up the worker's case, and respond on the worker's behalf to any view expressed at the hearing. The union official (or work colleague) can also confer with the worker during the hearing. In addition, Acas regards it as good practice to allow the union official (or work colleague) to participate as fully as possible in the hearing, including asking witnesses questions.

Those managers who move across to the public sector, or who join larger employers where unions continue to have a presence, can find the transition difficult. If their knowledge is based on the stereotypes portrayed in the media, then it can be no surprise if some are suspicious or even hostile to trade unions and find collective bargaining an alien concept. Suspicion breeds suspicion: the WERS Survey identified that where managers had a positive attitude to trade unions, there was more likely to be a relationship of trust. And, as these new managers arrive, experienced negotiators (both management and trade union) are leaving the profession, taking their hard-won skills with them.

This book is written with these new managers in mind, although I hope that new employee representatives, as well as experienced negotiators on both sides of the table, will find it of interest.

2

WHAT IS NEGOTIATING?

"Negotiating means getting the best of your opponent."
Marvin Gaye

This chapter defines what we mean by negotiation and contrasts it with a number of alternative ways of dealing with conflict in the workplace.

The first question a manager is likely to consider when engaging with a trade union on an issue is 'do I need to negotiate'? The matter in hand may not be appropriate to negotiations; perhaps it is something that you may wish to get the other side's views on but you don't need their agreement. Alternatively, perhaps even this is unnecessary, and all that is needed is for you to tell them what you have decided. Text books usually say that managers shouldn't negotiate unless they have to, and then only if it benefits management. This may be so, but a refusal to engage with your employees and their representatives may well have consequences for the relationship and for employment relations in the future.

To help make this decision it can be useful to look at the meaning of the competing processes open to managers and employee representatives. A good place to start is the Employee Involvement Continuum.

The employee involvement continuum

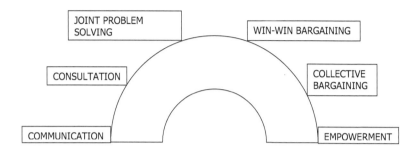

Fig. 1

This diagram represents the different processes used to involve employees, and their representatives, in decision-making in the workplace. As we shall see, moving from left to right along the spectrum represent a qualitative change in the decision-making process. Put simply, the continuum moves from briefing through listening to problem-solving, win-win bargaining, traditional collective bargaining and, finally, empowerment. Let's start by attempting to define some of these terms.

Communication:

"Is the provision and exchange of information and instructions which enable an organisation to function efficiently and employees to be properly informed about developments."
'Employee communication and consultation' Acas Booklet (June 2005)

Consultation:

"Is the process by which management and employees or their representatives jointly examine and discuss issues of mutual concern. It involves seeking acceptable solutions to problems through a genuine exchange of views and information."
'Employee communication and consultation' Acas Booklet (June 2005)

Joint Problem-Solving:

Is a collaborative process by which managers and employees work together to resolve conflict by defining and analysing a problem before generating options for its solution. Agreement is reached through consensus and the process therefore relies on sharing information and mutual trust.

Win-Win Bargaining:

Pioneered by Roger Fisher and William Ury in their 1983 book *Getting to Yes: Negotiating Agreement Without Giving In*, Win-Win Bargaining is a set of joint problem-solving techniques aimed at reaching agreement based on agreed principles, and not through the exercise of bargaining power. This is achieved by the parties being open about their interests; jointly developing a range of options; and assessing these against an agreed set of objective standards. It assumes that both parties can win because the process seeks to expand what is available to be shared rather than negotiate over a proscribed pot. Therefore, whilst in traditional bargaining the two sides compete to obtain their position, using the Win-Win approach, the parties collaborate to reach an agreement that satisfies both their interests.

Collective Bargaining:

"Is the process by which employers and recognised trade unions seek to reach agreement through negotiation on issues such as pay and terms and conditions of employment...both employer and trade union take responsibility for fulfilling the bargain."
'Employee communication and consultation' Acas Booklet (June 2005)

Empowerment:

Is the process whereby employees, or their representatives, are given the authority that enables them to control an aspect of the working life. To be meaningful, this autonomy must come with sufficient training, resources, budget, etc.

Moving from left to right on the Employee Involvement Continuum involves management increasingly giving up control on the outcomes of the processes. For example, communication can mean little more than a manager telling an employee representative something. Questions may be asked and answered, but the provision of information does not, in itself, involve the representative in decision-making. Communication may simply serve to inform that a decision has been made or, indeed, already implemented. Information provision may however be a necessary precursor to consultation, problem-solving or bargaining.

Moving to the next point on the continuum, consultation should mean, as a minimum, that employee representatives views are sought prior to a decision being made, leaving open the possibility at least that the eventual outcome can be affected by these discussions. Thus, employee representatives have the potential to persuade the decision makers and influence the outcome, but the final decision rests with management (a point returned to below). Properly, consultation should be a genuine discussion about the various options available, with the intention that this will inform the decision-making process and ensure that a better decision is made.

Collaborative forms of employee involvement such as joint problem-solving and Win-Win Bargaining can be viewed as investing in the employer-employee relationship. Some commentators and practitioners see this as the pinnacle of employee involvement and link it to the concept of partnership between employees and employers in the workplace. A key benefit of this approach is said to be employee engagement, which in turn leads to greater organisational efficiency and competitiveness; raised staff morale, motivation and discretionary effort; enhanced employee relations; and, the better management of change.

But Collective Bargaining is different. It goes beyond a commitment to work together because it involves the joint regulation of employees' terms and conditions of employment. It therefore requires an employer to accept that the union has a legitimate role to play in the workplace; it is in effect power sharing.

Collective Bargaining has been much maligned for its adversarial nature. In reality, however, it has more in common with joint problem-solving than is often recognised. Negotiation is not a simple espousal of positions: threats and exchanges of offers, followed by adjournments, and then by further counter-offers. Such manoeuvrings are time consuming and recipes for conflict and impasse. To work, negotiation must involve questioning and probing to uncover the parties' needs and interests. Listening has to be followed by genuine attempts to develop options. Offers need to be packaged to reflect the other side's concerns. Coercion will have a part to play but so will persuasion, movement and concession.

Moving to the end of the spectrum, genuine empowerment in employee relations is hard to find. In the past, trade unions have taken control of certain activities in the workplace. Overtime rosters were sometimes left to the local union officers to organise. In the print industry, the main union acted as an employment agency for its members. In more recent times, the involvement of employee representatives in this manner is likely to be restricted to the professions (for example medicine and the law) where professional bodies do not attract the opprobrium usually reserved for trade unions. However, the delegation of responsibility direct to employees does take place, particularly in the engineering industry, where semi-autonomous work groups are used to introduce greater flexibility and job enlargement/enrichment. Such examples may be few and far between, but they do illustrate the point that, in these limited circumstances and for specific purposes, employee empowerment can decentralise decision-making in the workplace.

The employee involvement continuum provides a useful overview, but reality is rarely that neat. In practice, the boundaries between these processes can cause problems for managers and employee representatives, not least because they come at them from different perspectives.

Am I negotiating or am I consulting?

It is perhaps not surprising that there is confusion over the distinction between consultation and negotiation. Indeed, this confusion can be deliberate. Typically, managers will seek to inform and, if necessary, consult on everything: they will try to limit the scope for negotiation and thereby restrict trade union input on decision-making. By contrast, unions will seek to expand the scope of negotiation, with consultation always seen as a poor second best. One local union official was honest enough to say to me that he would try and negotiate on everything, even when the procedural agreement said consultation was the appropriate process. It is interesting to note that the Workplace Employment Relations Survey 2004 found that, where trade unions were present, employee involvement was *"... weighted towards the 'negotiation end' of joint regulation compared to non-union employee representation which was more likely to be associated with information provision and consultation."*

This contrast in attitudes is not surprising as it reflects a fundamental difference between the two processes: in negotiation management and employee reps seek a joint determination of an issue whereas, in consultation, management retain the right to make the final decision.

Some experts will say that procedural agreements contribute to this confusion, as disputes procedures often allow for 'failure to agree' on matters that are clearly specified as consultation issues. The implication here is that, even if it is an issue for consultation, and not negotiation, the agreement of the other side and not just their views is being sought. Other practitioners will argue that this is better than leaving an issue unresolved, with no machinery for its resolution, because excluding some issues from procedures will only cause them to fester and reappear as disputes.

The confusion between consultation and negotiation is reflected in current employment law. The only legal definition of consultation is in the Trade Union Reform and Employment Rights Act (TURERA) 1993, which says that consultation with trade unions on redundancies should be conducted with *"a view to reaching agreement"*. On this point, the Act is the embodiment of a European Directive, so perhaps something was lost in translation, because this definition is difficult to distinguish from negotiation.

Employee reps may well disagree, but the best advice for managers is nevertheless to try to keep clear water between the two activities. Some procedural agreements attempt to do this by specifying which matters will be the subject of negotiation (for example, pay, hours of work, holiday entitlement); and what will be for consultation (for example, staffing levels, redundancies, work rosters). When a matter comes up for discussion, management can then be explicit about the process in which they will be engaging with the trade union, and act accordingly. An example of this 'two lists approach' is given below. The allocation of issues for consultation or negotiation shown here suited the organisation concerned but should not necessarily be regarded as good practice.

Issue	Consultation	Negotiation
Allowances		✓
Basic Pay		✓
Business Planning	✓	
Discretionary Benefits	✓	
Discipline & Grievance Procedure		✓
Equal Opportunities	✓	
Health & Safety	✓	
Holidays		✓
Hours of work		✓
Job Descriptions	✓	
Job Evaluation	✓	
Merit Pay		✓
Redundancies	✓	
Staffing Levels	✓	
Work Rosters		✓

Fig. 2

However, it is not always that simple, and managers need to be pragmatic. Issues arise which do not fit neatly into any prearranged list and no list can be exhaustive. What happens when a new subject comes up? What happens if something doesn't fit wholly into either category? For example, management may wish to introduce an allowance to encourage employees to engage in a new work activity by compensating them for travel costs they would otherwise incur. However, allowances may previously have not been regarded as a negotiable item and in the past have been treated as distinct from pay. What should the company do?

This may be an occasion when, even if the procedure says it is for consultation, it will be expedient to negotiate. This is because items for consultation can still form part of a contract of employment. It is a fact rarely admitted by managers, but negotiation allows for change in the workplace to be handled effectively. Collective bargaining with a recognised trade union can be an efficient way of changing employees' individual contracts of employment. Without the agreement of a trade union, managers are best advised to talk directly with each affected employee and seek their individual agreement. Where this is not forthcoming, contracts will need to be terminated, with notice, and new ones issued with the required changes included. But, such actions will be dismissals, with the potential at least for the employees concerned to seek legal redress. It can be much simpler and quicker to negotiate contractual changes with the recognised trade union.

The reality is that, whilst most text books will say that negotiation and consultation are separate processes, it can be hard always drawing a clear dividing line. Managers and trade unions will come at this from different angles, and this is understandable. What is important, however, is that disputes over process must be avoided at all cost. Disagreements in the workplace over substantive issues are to be expected and machinery should be put in place to deal with them. But, if the parties disagree over the procedures, and how they should operate, then the prospect for dispute resolution is bleak. For this reason, however imperfect definitions and procedures may be, they are needed, and all concerned must be pragmatic in their interpretation and application.

So, if the distinction between consultation and negotiation causes problems, why don't we all adopt a Win-Win approach? It certainly has its supporters: the IPA (the Involvement & Participation Association) campaigns tirelessly for employee involvement, consultation and partnership in the workplace, and Acas staff facilitate numerous joint working exercises every year. So why do we persist with traditional collective bargaining?

If traditional, adversarial, positional or distributive bargaining (the terms are interchangeable) is portrayed erroneously as the crude use of industrial muscle to get your own way, integrative bargaining, mutual gain bargaining, win-win negotiating or joint problem-solving (again the terms can effectively be regarded as interchangeable) has a softer, more modern, positive, "alternative dispute resolution" image. Its proponents claim that, with Win-Win bargaining, principles replace the exercise of power in the decision-making process. For some, therefore, it has an almost moral imperative.

But, perhaps surprisingly, joint problem-solving/win-win bargaining is not universally popular, amongst either managers or union representatives. A hard-nosed manager will see it as compromising 'management's right to manage'. They are responsible to the Board and the shareholders, and any dilution of their duty to run the business is unacceptable.

To a traditional union negotiator steeped in the ways of adversarial bargaining, joint problem-solving is a trick to lure the employee rep away from their proper role as opposition. Too much co-operation with management will undermine the union's ability to mobilise its members into taking coercive action when it is needed and, without this potential threat, the union would be powerless. After all, as has been said to me, "how do I know that I have done the best for my members if I haven't taken the employer to the wire on every issue?"

A cynical employee view of joint problem-solving techniques is that the emphasis on consensus, rather than on bargaining, is a cunning way of contaminating unions with the process. By participating, employee reps find that they are parties to unpopular decisions, which their members may have wanted opposed or their impact minimised.

For example, managers may invite employee reps to discuss how a redundancy selection policy will apply in a particular situation. The process will be described as problem-solving rather than negotiating. The aim will be to produce agreed protocols that are underpinned by shared values. The Union may well respond that, whilst they are prepared to negotiate the terms of a redundancy policy, their duty is to defend the interests of its members, not help to identify who should lose their job. In any redundancy selection process there will be winners and losers and it is the Union's job to support all its members. So, if the Union' agrees' to the redundancy selection process, they may feel constrained when defending members who subsequently lose their jobs. Union representatives have thus been contaminated by the process. On the other hand, if the Union agree to participate, their members are more likely to be treated fairly. Not only will the Union be able to influence the level of payouts, but it will be able to affect how the procedure is operated.

Neither point of view is 'right'. Different union officers will have different views, but managers seeking to use joint problem-solving techniques in these situations should appreciate the dilemmas union negotiators can face.

Win-Win bargaining can be harder than traditional bargaining. It requires trust. Negotiators fear that, if they open up and show their hand, they will lose out. It can feel safer and easier to stick to the known positions and rituals of adversarial bargaining. Don't forget, even if the negotiators are comfortable with an integrative approach, their constituents may well be less sophisticated; they may well expect their representatives to be robust in arguing their corner, not collaborating with the 'enemy'.

In its purest form, traditional bargaining is 'distributive', in that the assumption is that it is a zero-sum game. In other words, the 'pot' over which you are negotiating is limited, so that anything they win, you lose. By contrast, win-win bargaining is 'integrative'. A basic tenet is that it is possible to expand the 'pot'; both sides get more so that both sides' interests can be met. It is a win-win outcome.

However, this is something of a false divide, as even 'old school' adversarial negotiators should be alert to opportunities to expand the pot. Sometimes called 'gain sharing', many traditionally bargained productivity deals have been concluded on just this basis. If a deal can be constructed that increases productivity, then the profits that are generated can be shared between the employees and the shareholders. The possibility of increasing the size of the pot does not however necessarily resolve the problem. How this gain will be shared is likely to be the subject of adversarial bargaining.

It also has to be questioned whether a win-win outcome is always possible. A case in point is where the negotiations concern deterioration in employees' terms and conditions. In my experience, it is easier to find common ground when the negotiations are about 'gain-sharing' in the good times, but far more difficult if it is 'pain-sharing' when business is bad. So, if for example a manager is required to push through reductions in sick pay entitlement, longer not shorter working hours, or a worsening of pension rights, then a win-win outcome can be impossible. The best deal achievable is likely to be a 'not so good win' and a 'less-worse' lose. Adversarial bargaining may lend itself more readily to such situations. However, that does not mean that coercion, be that imposition or strike action, is inevitable. Traditional bargaining, done well, can be an effective way of managing conflict and introducing change even when trading conditions are poor.

Win-Win good, Traditional Bargaining bad?

Writing in the mid-60s, Walton and McKersie developed opposing distributive and integrative models of bargaining. They defined distributive bargaining as an approach which is based on the assumption that one party can only gain at the expense of the other, and, for that reason, it is fundamentally competitive. By contrast, integrative bargaining assumes that, if both negotiators are prepared to be open with each other and work together co-operatively, a solution can be found to reconcile their competing interests to their mutual gain. This is a useful model but, as Ray Fells, Lecturer in Organisational and Labour Studies at the University of Western Australia, has identified:

> "Negotiators do not engage solely in distributive or in integrative bargaining. In simple terms they do it all, perhaps using more

of one than the other on any particular occasion, but they will commit themselves to firm positions (distributive) yet explore options (integrative), make threats (distributive) and yet trust the other negotiator (integrative). To the extent that they develop a coherent strategy they may well seek to explore and expand the scope of joint gain before sorting out who gets what. In Walton and McKersie's terms, their bargaining will be mixed."

Raymond Friedman, author of *Front Stage, Back Stage: The Dramatic Structure of Labour Negotiations,* identified the shortcomings of traditional bargaining: excessive conflict; lack of negotiator involvement (meaning all but the lead negotiators actively participate); a high potential for misunderstanding; and, difficulty finding creative alternatives. All this is true, though I suggest that, done well, such shortcomings can be addressed by embracing negotiating best practice rather than by a wholesale rejection of traditional bargaining. Even Friedman had to admit that there is a lack of evidence that *"...interventions designed to create more integrative bargaining produces outcomes."* For me at least, he not only fails to persuade that it is possible *"...to break out of the rituals of negotiation"* but, more fundamentally, that there is a coherent and realistic alternative to be attained.

Over-reliance on adversarial bargaining techniques undoubtedly is destructive, both for the management/employee representative relationship and for the wider organisation. Not everything in the workplace can or should be negotiable, and consultation and joint problem-solving are the better ways forward in the appropriate circumstances. But, for me, pure Win-Win bargaining is too idealistic and its wholesale pursuit likely to be fruitless in all but a very few limited situations. Many have pursued this chimera but with little, if any, lasting success. A synthesis of the two approaches, with their techniques selected and applied appropriately to the situation in hand, is far more likely to be successful.

The manner in which these alternatives were presented by Walton and McKersie made it inevitable that the integrative approach would be seen as preferable. Indeed, there appears to be an unspoken presumption that integrative bargaining is inherently of greater moral worth; a mind-set which is shared by many of its latter-day adherents. I fear that a major part of this is an unwillingness to accept that modern workplaces are pluralistic, that sometimes conflict is inevitable and that trade unions have a valid role to play. The views of employee representatives may not always make easy listening for managers, and reps may not always voice the views of their various constituents as clearly and as accurately as they might. None of this however should mean that managers should stop listening.

Traditional negotiators can certainly learn lessons from and benefit by using Win-Win bargaining techniques. What is more, in some situations, an integrative approach is not only possible but preferable. So, the two approaches to negotiating, if used appropriately, can be complementary and the most successful negotiators I have seen in action use a mixture of integrative and distributive techniques. I have sought to outline their best practice in this book.

No doubt interest in Win-Win bargaining will continue to grow. Nevertheless, traditional collective bargaining will remain as the default method by which employers and employee representatives engage with each other because both managers and unions feel comfortable with it. This is not a bad thing. Used properly, traditional, adversarial bargaining can be an effective method of resolving conflict and managing change. But managers and employee representatives need to learn how to do it well and the best way to do this is to see negotiation as a process.

The process of a negotiation

Let's start with a traditional negotiation over a collective issue. All negotiations may be different: the power dynamics will vary, the personalities involved can change, but workplace negotiations do have features in common. This section provides a simple four stage structure which tracks the course of a typical employer/employee negotiation. Each stage comes with a number of logical steps and includes practical suggestions as to how these can be completed.

The aim of this structure is to help negotiators keep track of where they are in the process. As in comedy, timing in a negotiation is everything. Acting prematurely, trying to move too quickly, will only confuse and cause breakdown. Of course, negotiations rarely go as planned and it may be necessary to pause, and go back a stage, before moving forward towards settlement. But following this structure will maximise your chances of getting the deal you need.

The four stages are:

1. Preparation: "Doing your homework."

This stage involves intelligence gathering; analysis and assessment; advice on how to draw up a negotiating plan; best practice on team selection and organisation; as well as thoughts on choosing the venue for the negotiations.

2. Opening moves: "Setting out your stall."

Stage 2 starts with 'first impressions' as you walk into the negotiating room. It deals with the practicalities of listening to the other side and observing their behaviour. It then gives advice on the delivery of your opening presentation, followed by suggesting best practice on how you should question and probe your opponent's initial position. Finally, it deals with signalling, by which you can start to find a way forward.

3. Middle game: "From proposing to hard bargaining."

The third stage deals with movement; how to get movement and how to respond by making appropriate concessions. Following on from this is option generation, which allows the eventual shape of the deal to start to take shape. Included in this stage is practical advice on two techniques that are needed at this point: how to summarise and how to use adjournments. Also dealt with here are threats, coercion & the application of pressure – not only how to respond, but how to do it.

4. End game: "Closing the deal."

The final stage gives help with closing the deal and says how to deal with a suggestion that you should 'split the difference'. It deals with writing up and signing off before discussing the often overlooked implementation phase. Also included are suggestions for reviewing your performance.

In the next four chapters we will look at each of these stages in turn in some detail. Reality is rarely that straightforward but, as long as you have a clear understanding of where you are in the process, even if all does not go to plan, if you follow these stages (to misquote Mick Jagger) you may not always get all of what you want, but you should get what you need.

3

PREPARING FOR A NEGOTIATION

"My Lord, I have a cunning plan."
Baldrick, to Edmund Blackadder

"By failing to prepare, you are preparing to fail."
Benjamin Franklin (1706 – 1790)

In negotiation, as in any business activity, preparation is essential. This chapter sets out what can be done before the talks get underway to improve your chances of getting a good deal.

Intelligence gathering

Firstly, there is intelligence gathering: what do you already 'know' about the coming talks and what can you find out? What do you know about the personalities, their aspirations and their needs? You may already have received their 'shopping list', but what lies behind this? What can you reliably interpret from this regarding their intentions? In doing this it may be useful to explore informal contacts with the other side. For example, it is common practice for there to be contacts at a lower level in an organisation between front line managers and local employee reps; can these sources cast any light on what is to come?

Managers should have their own networks that provide them with a feel for what the workforce is thinking. This should provide an indication of how seriously the Union will pursue its negotiating agenda. In particular, is there likely to be widespread support for industrial action should an agreement not be readily achieved through bargaining? More than this, would that support remain there for a sustained campaign? A word of warning: employees often say different things to different audiences. A union officer can be told that the members are up for a fight, whilst a manger can be told quite the opposite by the same people. This dissonance can lead managers to underestimate the strength of feeling amongst the workforce. Even the results of so called 'indicative ballots' cannot be relied upon, so experienced negotiators often wait for the outcome of a formal industrial action ballot before assuming too much.

I was once asked, "How do you spot hidden agendas?" The answer, of course, was "you can't, that's why they are hidden". Nevertheless, if you use your experience and informal contacts, you can make some intelligent guesses. But, always remember that you are making assumptions, so beware simply attributing your worst fears as the motivation for the other side's behaviour.

There may be harder data available. It may be that you operate in an industry that provides data that can be used in the forthcoming discussions. For example, some trade organisations collect information on pay settlements; is there a 'going rate'? You may have contacts in similar organisations that deal with the same trade union: how did the local Full-time Officer behave in their last pay talks? Are there lessons to be learned or experiences that can be shared? It may be that the Union is currently pursuing a new policy, will this impact on your negotiations?

If you have had experience of past negotiations with the other side, this will bring with it the ability to put yourself in their shoes. Empathy can provide valuable insights, especially if you know the personalities involved. In doing this you need to be aware of the danger of attributing your deepest fears to their intentions and motivations. If we assume the worst, and treat the other side accordingly, they will immediately pick up on this negativity, and your fears will become a self-fulfilling prophecy. So, before making unfounded assumptions, use your sources to check the facts.

It is inevitable in a negotiation that you concentrate on what you have in difference with the other side. However, in your preparation, it is also useful to consider what have you in common. This can then be used in a number of ways and at appropriate points in the negotiations. For example, it can be used to reduce tension when the negotiations seem to heading towards deadlock, as a timely reminder that you aren't in disagreement about everything. It can help to put your differences into perspective and get momentum going again in the talks. Reflecting on what you have in common can also help when preparing your case. Using shared values and areas of agreement when presenting your arguments can encourage the other side to be more open to alternative views and look at your proposals more positively. But don't be surprised when they don't immediately see it all your way.

Analysis

The next step is analysis, and there are three dimensions you need to consider: Features (what you will be bargaining over); Factors (how you can modify what you are bargaining over); and, Positions (what you would like, realistically want & must have).

Both sides will come to the negotiations with their wants and needs which can take the form of a lengthy 'shopping list' of claims. This is the 'what' of the negotiations. For progress to be made agreement will be needed (implicit or explicit) on what will be the subject on the negotiations; in effect this is an agenda for the discussions, although, this agenda can itself be the subject of bargaining as the negotiations progress.

Furthermore, negotiators need to be aware that what you will be negotiating over will not always be apparent from the outset. Sometimes, early communications between the parties can reveal what is really in contention (and this can be worth exploring in a pre-negotiation, informal stage), but it still may not become clear until the negotiations are underway. The 'presenting issues' may not be the underlying issues, either because this is a deliberate tactic or possibly because the other side are confused as to their real aims. Questioning and probing will be needed to reveal the true position once the negotiating starts.

Secondly, you will need to consider the range of inter-dependent factors (cost, timescales, contractual entitlements, etc.) that can be modified to shape the eventual deal. Bargaining is essentially an attempt to vary and trade these parameters until a package can be agreed in a form that is acceptable to all concerned. In practice this can make the negotiations very complex.

As the talks progress negotiators make a series of offers and then respond with counter-offers. In doing so, the factors fluctuate, with all the elements interacting to affect the worth of the prospective deal. Needless to say, the 'worth' of the deal on offer is in the eye (or to be more accurate, the pocket) of the beholder. For example, cost and time can be flexed: management might go for a phased or a back-loaded deal, if the full cost does not come in for some months or years, and changes in working practices introduced immediately. Employee reps are more likely to seek immediate payment, with any contractual changes made at a later date.

Many deals are done not by some master stroke of inspiration, but rather by repackaging an existing offer in a way that is more palatable to the other side. But to do this you need to know, and have costed, the factors involved.

Nor should it be assumed that the parties will be entirely rational in their calculations. There is a magic in numbers that convey significance beyond their actual worth. Thus a goal of a 5% increase can mean that compromise, even at 4.99%, will prove disproportionately difficult to achieve! Part of the problem here is the aspirations of the parties and the mandates they have set their negotiators. Their leaders may have led them up the hill, only to find it far more difficult to lead them back down again. Elements of a claim can therefore have a totemic value that can be hard for the other side to comprehend fully. Indeed, the significance can have deep roots. However, this can play to your advantage: never forget that you should not only calculate the value of a deal to you, but also consider what the value of the deal will be to them.

I have been involved in many deals where lump sum buy-outs were used to get a workforce to agree to reductions in their contractual entitlements. This is a very effective way for managers to 'buy' change. Employees tend to be very receptive to such offers, even though over time they will lose out. An upfront payment is a benefit of value to them. However, to an employer it can be a cheap offer to make because they can take a longer view. The change may continue to save the employer money, possibly for many years to come, and this can be achieved for a relatively modest outlay which is recoverable in the medium term. The two parties have a different attitude to timescales and therefore they value the deal differently.

Case Study 1

Some years ago (and before the introduction of legislation on working hours) I was involved in a dispute a medium sized manufacturing company. As part of the annual pay negotiations, management wanted to achieve productivity savings by the removal of paid tea breaks. The union negotiator was very reluctant to agree because he saw this as deterioration of terms and conditions of employment which it had taken the union many years to achieve. His view was that the workforce should resist any such attempt.

Management persisted and, as the negotiations progressed, it became clear to me that the union negotiator was being pressed by his own side to agree to a buy-out. Unfortunately for him, management had good intelligence that the workforce would be amenable to a relatively low offer.

Management's final pay offer included a one-off payment costed on the basis that employees would receive lump-sum equivalent to the pay they would have received for tea breaks in 6 months period. The union negotiator felt obliged to put this to ballot where it was accepted overwhelmingly by the workforce.

Whilst the employees benefitted from receiving what was a significant amount of money in a lump-sum, the company recouped this in savings on the pay bill in a very short timeframe and were able to use the ongoing cost reductions to in part offset the cost of the annual pay increase.

So, in preparing for a negotiation, every item on the shopping list will need to be assessed to give the overall worth of a proposed deal. Furthermore, every offer and counter-offer will need to be costed and re-costed as the negotiations progress. It is sensible therefore to anticipate this at this stage and, if possible, produce sliding scales, contingency tables, spread sheets, etc., to enable you to respond quickly and confidently to the other side's changing demands.

Thought also should be given to power relationships in your organisations. All organisations are pluralistic, with power not simply concentrated at the top but spread, to varying degrees, across it. For this reason, all organisations are political with a small 'p'. When going into a negotiation, you are negotiating on behalf of 'your side'; but what does 'your side' mean? You and your team will reflect a coalition of interests and team members need to be selected to reflect those interests. Furthermore, there needs to be consensus within the team and amongst your constituents on what you are seeking and what will be acceptable.

Of course, not all your constituents will have an equal say. The negotiating team needs a leader who is to be seen to have status in the organisation and who has been given the authority to negotiate within a mandate. But powerful constituents will be outside of the negotiating team. The Chief Executive or the Managing Director may well make the final decision; but, if IT hate it and says the system won't cope with it, or if the Production Manager says it is unworkable, will the deal stick? And, if it doesn't, what will that do to your position and to future negotiations? The worst of all worlds is to reach an agreement that can't be delivered.

An important part of your preparation (and one that is often overlooked) is getting an achievable and sufficiently flexible mandate from your constituents. It is rare for any manager or union officer to go into a negotiation with a free hand. No matter how senior they may be, they will have constituents whose views they need to represent. It is therefore essential that, as negotiator, you are confident in your mandate and have the authority to negotiate.

In effect this can be a negotiation within a negotiation. As a negotiator you need to know exactly what you can and can't do to get a deal. It can be hard for a manager to explain to a Chief Executive (or a union officer to persuade the branch executive) that what they want you to get can't be done, at least not without a cost they will not want to pay. Yet it is better for the Chief Executive (and the branch) to accept the reality of the situation before the negotiations begin than to have to make an embarrassing climb down later on. And it may well be you not them that gets the blame!

But sadly, management and union negotiators all too often go into negotiations with unrealistic and over-aspirational objectives set for them. As a result, they are often forced to go back and get a revised mandate from their masters – a point that may well not be missed by those on the other side of the negotiating table. To avoid this, you need to have a confidential communication channel, established in advance; but use it sparingly and, ideally, without the other side being aware of its existence. As the talks continue you will come under pressure. Can you offer something further? Can you extend your 'bottom line'? You are likely to need to shift your position to get a deal but, as we will see, too much movement, made too quickly, will cause you problems. The more you can do to anticipate and plan for such contingencies will stand you in good stead later on.

What is more, consensus in your team can be fragile when put under pressure, so during adjournments you will need to make sure that all on your side remain signed up to your strategy as the negotiation progresses. Again, indentifying such problems in advance can help you deal with such problems when they arise. One consolation is that the 'other side' facing you across the table will also be coalition of differing, and sometimes conflicting, interest groups, so they are likely to be experiencing similar problems.

Positions

The next step is to consider what position you should adopt, at least initially. To do this requires an assessment of what you want and, perhaps more importantly, what you will need from the negotiations. In essence, this is about prioritisation. You need to be clear as to **what, ideally, you would like**; realistically, **what you want** to achieve; and, as a bottom line, **what you must get** to meet your needs.

Your ideal position will be your opening position. By trading concessions, you can expect to move slowly towards your realistic position. Your intention will be to settle as close to your ideal position as possible; however, whilst they might not express it in these terms, your opponents will be doing a similar assessment but from their perspective. If, as the negotiations progress, questioning and probing reveal that your respective bottom lines overlap, then a deal should be achievable.

Below is a simple diagram (Fig. 3) which illustrates this point. The 'area for movement' shown by the double-headed arrow will be the territory over which the bargaining can be expected to take place. In this scenario, neither party are likely to achieve either their ideal position or even their realistic position. It would seem that even the parties' respective bottom line positions barely overlap, so the negotiators will have to work hard to get one (or more likely both) of the sides to move.

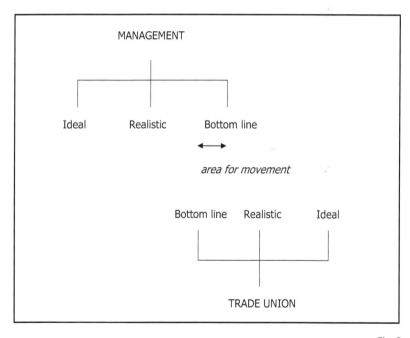

Fig. 3

But, what happens when the two bottom lines do not overlap and neither party are able to move? The answer is deadlock. Before entering any negotiations, therefore, you need to know what your true bottom line is, because you are either going to have to stick to it or go back to your constituents and get a revised mandate (and nobody likes to do that too often as it calls into question your ability as a negotiator). And, as we shall see later, too much movement (and too many 'final' offers) weakens your credibility.

When deciding your bottom line, it will help if you also consider what your 'Best Alternative to a Negotiated Agreement' (often referred to as a BATNA) might be. A BATNA is both an alternative to negotiation (you have somewhere else to go), for example you can walk away from the negotiation or you can impose; and, it is a strong negotiating advantage (the other side knows you have somewhere else to go) and can be used to put pressure on the other side in a negotiation. If the other side know that you don't need to reach an agreement with them because you have an alternative way forward, it puts you in a powerful position, but watch out, it can escalate the conflict. They may have a BATNA too! But, you may not have an option, so, as Ashleigh Brilliant, the author, cartoonist and professional epigrammatist says,

"If you can't go around it, over it, or through it, you had better negotiate with it"

The negotiating lan

Having established your opening position, together with what you realistically think you can achieve, and your bottom line (including, whenever possible, a 'Plan B', which is what your alternative to a negotiated settlement might be), you can now produce a plan for the negotiations.

As Dwight D. Eisenhower put it (and my former Chief Executive was fond of quoting), *"Plans are nothing; planning is everything."* The only certainty is that the negotiations will not go to plan, but planning will give you a place to start and help you deal with the unexpected.

Your negotiating plan should include:

- A factual summary of the situation together with background briefing materials (you should already have this from your information gathering exercise).

- Objectives for the coming negotiations. In doing this, you need not only to think about the short and immediate term, but also about the wider picture. How will these negotiations and your objectives for them, fit into the broader strategy of the organisation? Is there, for example, a Human Resources strategy already in place and, if so, how will these negotiations fit in with it? When the negotiations start, you will need to be able to keep these objectives in mind, even when dealing with the details.
- The arguments you will use to support your case (you can use your analysis to develop these). But don't place too much faith in the power of logical argument: negotiating is rarely just a rational debate! Remember the emotional appeal of your argument and build this into your thinking.
- What you predict the arguments of the other side will be and how you will counter them. To do this you will need to know the weaknesses, as well as the strengths, of your case. Many negotiators get over-enthusiastic about the strength of their case. They are convinced by the logic of their position and can be taken by surprise when the other side doesn't see it in the same way! The trick here is to see what you are proposing through the eyes of the other side, put yourself in their shoes and anticipate their response accordingly. A role I have often played when talking privately with one side is that of "devil's advocate". This can help negotiators evaluate their arguments constructively by looking at them from an opposing viewpoint.
- The tactics you will employ to pursue your case. You cannot know at the outset exactly how the negotiations will unfold; they are by their very nature dynamic and unpredictable But, you can plan, for example, how you will seek to put pressure on the other side, on which points you will move quickly for agreement and on which points you will hold out and play it long.

  One such tactic might be to start with relatively minor items, which would otherwise be dealt with once the main issues had been agreed. The idea is that, because these minor points should be easy to agree, this will give an impetus to the negotiations and build up the relationship, all of which should stand you in good stead when you come to more fundamental matters. Opening in this way can build momentum, but a cautious negotiator, when faced with such a tactic, will insist that any agreement on minor points is conditional on the major points being agreed. Everything has a cost.

- Too often in a dispute the first thing to fail is communications and yet, all too often, disputes degenerate into battles of press notices, with both sides seeking to occupy the moral high ground. If information is not released on the progress of the talks, news will get out, or be invented, to fill the vacuum. If managers don't brief their staff, the Union or the media will, so it is prudent to manage the process and involve your PR/Communications team from the outset of any negotiations.

Negotiations should be conducted in confidence, indeed privacy is essential if the parties are to be able to generate fresh ideas and explore new options. However, increasingly both employers and trade unions have recourse to the media to try and win the support of the workforce and of the wider public. The availability of modern communication media (mobile phones, texts, emails and the internet) mean that it is increasingly difficult to keep the talks private; even vows of silence seem rarely to work.

Far too frequently middle and line managers get left out of the loop. Indeed, it is not uncommon for local employee reps, although themselves not involved in the negotiations, to be better informed than their managers. Not surprisingly, their managers find this hard to take, especially as they know that, whatever comes out of the negotiations, it will fall to them to ensure its implementation.

Finally, there is both law and good practice when it comes to disclosing information to trade unions.

You need to consider therefore how and when you will communicate:

- Internally, with the workforce and your line managers
- Externally, with the media, should the negotiations become news-worthy
- With the other side, prior to and during the talks.

All of the above should form your negotiating plan which needs to be put together into a confidential brief for you and your negotiating team. There should then be a pre-meeting of your side, with sufficient time allowed to go through the brief, allocate roles and undertake further investigation and analysis should the need arise.

Team organisation

It is difficult, if not impossible, for one person to speak, listen, take notes, fully understand all aspects of their case, watch the other side's reactions and analyse how the talks are going. It is traditional, therefore, for a negotiating team to have a leader, a note-taker and a summariser (who is there to assess developments and report back to the team in adjournments); plus team members with specialist knowledge. Each one should know exactly what they are being asked to do. All team members need to be well briefed in advance of the negotiations and fully understand the mandate that has been given to the team.

Even with training, not everyone can be an effective negotiator, so it is worth picking your team with care. In reality, however, team membership is often dictated by the position the individuals hold, their availability and their specialist knowledge. Nevertheless, equally important should be a negotiator's ability to convey the right message by what they say and how they conduct themselves. If someone has to be there because of the job they hold, consider getting them trained in negotiation and communication skills.

Your choice of team members will send a message to the other side, and, when there is a dispute in progress, much will be read into their selection. This can partly be attributed to the fevered atmosphere of a dispute, when, like Kremlin-watchers of the Cold War years, every minor change was picked up on and its implications pored over. However, there is some sense in it: personalities will be big influence on how the talks are likely to progress, so who is on the opposing team will be significant and their inclusion might say something about the power balance of the other side. You need to have someone with real authority on your side of the table and you will look to see if there is a decision maker or opinion former on their side. Both sides will be thinking, 'are they here to negotiate or just talk?' You need to be able to show that you have the authority to do business.

As a rule of thumb, it is sensible to keep the size of your team as small as, and certainly no larger than, the opposition team. Firstly, because larger teams tend to be unwieldy; and, secondly, because having the larger team sends the wrong messages: it suggests, for example, that there are divisions on your side of the table and the key players cannot be trusted to negotiate by themselves. For these reasons, it is sensible therefore to consider how your team selection will play with the other side and use it as part of your negotiating plan.

A key consideration will be the choice of lead negotiator. Negotiating forums are notoriously status orientated. The seniority of the lead management negotiator can influence who leads on the union side. Thus, if the Managing Director leads for the company, the Union side is more likely to want to involve their Full-time Officer or even a National Officer. If the dispute is of national significance, Assistant General Secretaries or even General Secretaries are likely to become involved. A consideration is therefore the need to leave some headroom should negotiations fail. Commonly such decisions are dictated by the stage reached in the dispute procedure, but once this has become exhausted, it may still be prudent to hold your most senior player back so you can bring them in later. There are however problems associated by raising the stakes in this way and "bringing in the grandparents".

Whoever it is decided will lead, it is standard practice in traditional negotiating that the lead negotiator will do the talking and team members do not speak unless directly invited to do so by the leader. Their contribution should then be to speak only on the point currently under discussion and on which they have been briefed in advance.

Interrupting will disrupt the line being pursued by your lead negotiator, will weaken the case being developed and will look unprofessional. It may be however that a team member has spotted something or may feel that their leader is going off-message. In such situations a note should be passed to the leading negotiator asking for an urgent adjournment. Over-use of this tactic however will lead to stop-start negotiations and be counterproductive; it is therefore usually preferable to wait for a natural break in proceedings.

Negotiators will be conscious of the need to present a common front. In any team it is likely, however, that there will be disagreements over tactics or even over objectives. Keeping your own side in check and reining in the loose cannons in your team are problems that you don't need but all too often occur. Negotiators will normally want to maintain the illusion of complete consensus on their side of the table, whilst being on the look-out for divisions in the other side's camp. If conflicts between team members are spotted on the other side of the table, the usual response is to add your support to the moderate camp. This can work to your advantage in two ways: firstly, it increases their internal differences, and therefore reduces their effectiveness; and, secondly, it makes you appear to be less an opposing advocate, and puts you more in a judicial role, evaluating the situation in a neutral manner. Either way, exploiting the other sides' differences enhances your bargaining strength.

Of course, there may be occasions when outbursts from a team member will be deliberately staged, to demonstrate the strength of feeling within the team on a particular point. Playing to the gallery may be required to satisfy the internal politics of the team or be directed at stakeholders not even present. This tactic can also be a deliberate attempt to present the lead negotiator as a moderating influence. The intent here is to seek to discourage the other side from pressing too hard on the point, suggesting that, if they do, they will harden the position and strengthen the hand of the hawks on the other side of the table. As a negotiating tactic it is akin to the 'Good Cop, Bad Cop' ploy described in the chapter on Dirty Tricks. Alternatively, the outburst could be genuine and should therefore be taken very seriously. No one said negotiating was easy!

It should be noted that, whilst traditional bargaining can be little more than a dialogue between the two lead negotiators, the more integrative approach as practiced by proponents of Win-Win bargaining is far more inclusive. Here team members on both sides feel able to contribute to the discussions and the role of the lead negotiator becomes more of a co-ordinator. However, where feelings are running high, the negotiation meetings can degenerate into chaos. My view would be that a more democratic approach should only be encouraged when trust levels are high. Neither approach is necessarily 'wrong', but as ever, it is 'horses for courses'.

Note taking

Arrangements for minute or note taking vary. Few organisations these days keep verbatim records of proceedings. Some workplaces do however take a formal note of meetings. Some organisations, usually those in the public sector, produce formal minutes and agree these with the other side. Management generally provide secretarial support for this purpose. If this is the case, it is indeed sensible to have someone whose job it is to arrange meetings, agree agendas, circulate papers and generally maintain the paperwork.

The benefit of a formal note of the meeting being taken is more debatable. Such traditional meeting formalities can sit uneasily with the flow of collective bargaining. Part of the problem is that the process of agreeing the note as a true record acquires a life of its own. The wording of the note can itself become an issue for debate, with disputes over the meaning and implications of the words used. I would suggest that a better way forward is for the Chair of the meeting (generally the senior member of management present) to agree action points, either as the meeting progresses or at its end. However, it really is a matter of custom and practice.

In negotiations, it is generally thought good practice for both sides to have a note taker, although most negotiators will keep a few notes themselves. However, it is very difficult for a lead negotiator to speak, listen and plan their next intervention whilst, at the same time, taking notes. A note taker comes into their own in side-meetings, when team members will discuss what has been said and accurate notes will be invaluable aid to this process.

A distinction here can be drawn between regular, planned meetings of management and employee representatives, and one-off meetings dedicated to negotiation. The former type may lend itself to having an agreed note of proceedings more than the latter.

Agreeing the venue

This should not be allowed to be a contentious item! The choice of venue should encourage the negotiations to run as smoothly as possible. When the pressure is on, tempers can become frayed and minor irritations over the choice of venue or the facilities available can only add to the problem. Negotiation is difficult enough, without problems with the ventilation, or noise from the factory floor, interrupting proceedings.

It is possible that one side may seek an advantage by ensuring that the negotiations are held on their territory, with the "home team" having better facilities, larger, rooms or more prestigious accommodation. The intention is to put the other side on the back foot from the outset. Even the layout of the room can be used to give one side an advantage. Although inexperienced negotiators may feel unable to challenge such dirty tricks, once exposed such transparent practices will counterproductive. So, unless your intention is to provoke a walkout, or get the talks to break down before they have properly started, this is a tactic best avoided.

Case Study 2

I ran a negotiating training event for prison officers. The group was split into two, with those playing the managers remaining in the conference room where the exercise would be staged. I said that this group could set the room up as they wanted. They arranged the seating so that their side had higher chairs set closely together behind the negotiating table. By contrast, they positioned lower chairs, spread out, away from the table for the group playing the union side.

This was an obvious, but effective, trick that put the 'union side' at an immediate, psychological disadvantage; a fact that was not lost upon them. This was only a training exercise and it was done tongue-in-cheek, but it made a very good point: the layout of a venue affects how participants feel about the negotiation.

Some commentators have questioned the traditional layout of the negotiating room; participants sit in their teams on opposite sides of a large table, with their respective lead negotiators sitting directly opposite each other. This layout undoubtedly emphasises the formality and adversarial nature of traditional negotiation. I have experimented with different formats. For example, when facilitating joint problem-solving groups I have encouraged participants not to sit in their teams and used circular tables to encourage a less adversarial approach.

It is sometimes suggested that negotiators should use lower, armchairs, without the barrier of a table separating those involved. Wouldn't this make relationships feel less conflictual and encourage collaboration? This is possibly so, but there are a few practicalities that need to be taken into account. If the subject matter is likely to raise emotions, and the process you are in is traditional bargaining, sitting opposite each other across a table allows each side to share notes and pass information within the team in some privacy. What is more, negotiators like a table between them to allow them to spread out their papers. No doubt it is partly a matter of habit, but when I have tried to change this, those involved appeared most uncomfortable and I soon changed the layout back to a traditional format.

As a conciliator, I always preferred to sit at the head of suitably sized oblong table, with one team of negotiators down one side of the table and the other team along the opposite side facing them. This enabled me not only to maintain eye contact with the lead negotiators but also to note the body language displayed by their teams. As we shall see later, you can learn a lot from how people behave in a negotiation. For this reason, whenever possible, I would suggest that when you are negotiating try and position yourself so that you can observe both the reactions of the opposition and keep an eye on your own side.

The majority of employer/union negotiations are conducted on the employer's premises. There may however be occasions when the use of neutral territory is advisable. If the coming meeting is one of a series, and earlier meetings have not gone well, then a different venue can change the dynamic and encourage a different mindset.

Whether the meeting is at the workplace or at a local hotel, what will be needed is privacy. The main conference room will need to be plenty large enough for both teams to meet and should be laid out in conventional manner, with sufficient seating for all the members of the two teams to sit facing each other. There should also be at least two break-out rooms, sufficiently for each team to meet privately and out of earshot of the other team. It can also be prudent to have additional space available should it be necessary for the lead negotiators to meet separately. Ideally, side rooms should have internet access, with facilities for typing, photocopying and fax. If you anticipate that talks might over-run, make sure that these facilities are readily available night and day. There is nothing worse than having to relocate a meeting at short notice late in the day! It is also essential that access by members of the public (and in particular members of the press) is restricted, so security will be a factor in choosing a venue.

Consideration should also be given to providing refreshments. Unless you really want to make it a war of attrition, it is sensible to feed negotiators, because, needless to say, they will become irritable if you don't. There is a tradition in Acas National that fish and chips are provided for late night sessions. One of my first jobs was to go and get them. Indeed, on one occasion, a news reporter attempted to find out who was having what – it must have been a slow news day. There is however a serious purpose here: if negotiating teams go off site for a meal, negotiations will get delayed, lose impetus and probably stall. They will be lobbied by their constituents, interviewed by the media and, in all likelihood, attitudes will harden. I have to admit, that in those days, when drinking during the working day was far more common, it was also a way of keeping all concerned sober! It is also worth noting that, used well, offering coffee and handing around sandwiches can break the tension by bringing a degree of informality to the proceedings. A break can be used for a number of purposes and the use of adjournments is returned to later.

You might even wish to consider where harassed negotiators can go if they feel in need of a cigarette. It might seem a minor point, but if the meeting is on the 22nd floor (as the Acas conference rooms in London are), and you are dealing with confirmed nicotine addicts, you can guarantee that the day will be interrupted as members of both teams become unavailable at different times. It may seem obvious, but you should build in breaks and put deadlines on adjournments. What can make matters worse is that, whilst indulging their cravings, they may be outside talking to the press and fragmenting the negotiations. This happened to me in a local government dispute. At one point, I had separate talks going on in the main room and, simultaneously, amongst those standing outside the front entrance.

Next, clear you diary, and those of your team, for the whole day. There is nothing more irritating for the other side than to learn that, just when they thought progress was being made, you have other appointment to go to. It calls into question your sincerity and the importance you attach to resolving the issue. It is very hard to predict how long a negotiation will last. Late night meetings should certainly be avoided is at all possible (they are no way to make good decisions) but there will be times when they are necessary.

Talks about talks

Finally, be ready for a last minute hitch. Sometimes called 'talks about talks', you may find that some pre-negotiations are needed just to get the other side in the same room as you! This may simply be 'gamesmanship' on their part or it may indicate something more serious. Either way, don't react, ask questions and where appropriate remind them that the best way of resolving problems is to talk – so let's start talking.

One problem particularly common in the public sector and the not for profit sector is that union reps can question the authority of management; bypass them by going over their heads and appeal direct to the governing body. This can be a deliberate manoeuvre or it may be that the employee reps genuinely believe that, if they could only explain their case direct to the members of this body, the matter could be resolved. In effect, management are being treated as the problem. But, if this is allowed to happen, management's status as negotiators can be damaged beyond repair. Not only will it be difficult for management to recover from this position, but it will have set a dangerous precedent for future negotiations. It can be useful, should negotiations break down, for the governing body to get involved, but this must be at a later stage. Local management must be allowed to initiate negotiations and be given the authority to do their job.

There are however ways of dealing with it. Firstly, it can be provided for in the collective disputes procedure, which can be structured to allow one or more representatives of the governing body to chair the final internal stage. Secondly, an ad hoc arrangement can be adopted to allow this to happen as a one off. In either event, it is vital that the senior managers involved in the negotiation are not seen to be sidelined if they are to be able to do business with the employee reps again in the future.

So, preparation complete, you should now be ready to go into the negotiations. Hopefully, you will have stage-managed matters properly so that the forthcoming negotiations will be conducted in a constructive and positive manner. But be realistic – things rarely go entirely to plan. When former Prime Minister Harold Macmillan was asked what had thwarted his best intentions, he is reported to have replied "Events, dear boy, events." Events will interfere with negotiation, so expect the unexpected!

4

OPENING MOVES

"There are four ways, and only four ways, in which we have contact with the world. We are evaluated and classified by these four contacts: what we do, how we look, what we say, and how we say it."
Dale Breckenridge Carnegie

This chapter describes what should be done to get negotiations off to the best possible start: we will explore how to make the opening moves from how to create positive first impressions, to ways of getting the discussions moving.

First impressions

The tone of a negotiation is set long before the first meeting. In employee relations, there will invariably have been an exchange of correspondence, emails, telephone calls or even informal meetings with trade union representatives. There may even have been earlier formal meetings as previous stages of a dispute or grievance procedure. Inevitably, the manner in which these exchanges were carried out will impact on the subsequent across-the-table negotiations. It is important therefore to conduct these in a professional manner. In particular, any correspondence will be scrutinised and analysed, so any perceived slight will be exaggerated and return to haunt the negotiations.

Before your team walks into the negotiating room, consider, 'how will we be perceived?' What unspoken messages are you as a team communicating? You and your team need to appear, relaxed, professional, and upbeat. Does your appearance match this message? Studies claim that over half of your message will be carried through non-verbal elements. Knowingly or unknowingly, your team's collective body language, appearance, eye contact, and facial expressions will all be saying things to the other side. As Peter Drucker puts it, *"The most important thing in communication is hearing what isn't said."*

How to communicate without even speaking

"O would some power the giftie gie us to
see ourselves as others see us."
Robert Burns

When you and your team walk into the negotiating room for the first time, consciously or not, the other side will be processing information about you; so make sure that these messages are consistent with what is intended. Come in together, but not having private conversations or sharing a joke. Remember, you are now on stage, so put a pleasant smile on your face (but not a fixed grin!) and look relaxed, even if you are not.

It starts with our appearance. How we dress will make an immediate impression, and stimulate both a conscious and unconscious reaction. The norms of business dress have changed over time and can vary significantly according to the culture of the organisation. So how you dress will show whether you want to fit in or not. It depends what message you want to send. If you decide to demonstrate your individuality by wearing clothes very different from the norm, the messages you send out will be confusing to your audience and this can unconsciously trigger their irritation. Generally, you will want to appear business-like but not a 'power-dresser'. Managers who appear over-formal will come over as wanting to emphasise their status; too casual and they will seem not to be treating the meeting with sufficient seriousness. So, give some thought to your appearance: consider how it will fit in with the meeting and reinforce the messages you want to send.

You can even use your team's collective appearance to make a point and emphasise your difference.

Case Study 3

I once was asked to facilitate a relationship-building day for the governor and union reps at a prison establishment. I had persuaded the Governor and his management team to allow this to be off-site. I thought I had also agreed with all concerned that the agreed dress code was to be informal. Certainly the Governor complied; he arrived in T-shirt and jeans. The Union side, however, turned out in full dress uniform.

The impact was striking. It was undoubtedly a 'dirty trick' and set the tone for the day, which was not a great success. But, I have to admit, it was a powerful way of indicating their view of the relationship.

As soon as we walk into a room, our posture, eye contact and facial expressions all send out non-verbal messages. When we do speak, the sound of our voice, its pitch and tone, pace of delivery, and intonation all convey information. All of these signals can actively support what we are saying or they can contradict our intended message. Added together, these project an image of you which can work to your advantage or your disadvantage.

Professor Albert Mehrabian is an authority on communications who came up with some remarkable statistics on the effectiveness of spoken communications:

- 7% of meaning is in the words that are spoken.
- 38% of meaning is paralinguistic (the way that the words are said).
- 55% of meaning is in facial expression.

The aim of this section is not to make your an expert in body language, but to provide negotiators with a basic introduction to this 93% of communication. If we can be aware of our body language, we can use it to enhance our communication skills. Not only that, but we can pick up on the unconscious messages others are sending.

I approach the subject body language with a degree of scepticism.

Firstly, because some of it seems to be the science of the obvious: if your opponent is frowning, it does not require any great analysis to identify that he or she may not be happy with what you are saying. Secondly, I remain unconvinced that some of it can be of practical assistance. I understand that a group of theories termed Neuro-Linguistic Programming is used by some negotiators. I have been told that these teach us that eye movement and pupil dilation provides insight into what someone is thinking. Apparently, those of us who tend to look to the right are more influenced by logic and precision, whereas left lookers are more emotional, subjective and suggestible. All of this may or may not be true but, unfortunately, my own eyesight is not sufficiently good enough to spot these small cues from the other side of a negotiating table.

Negotiators do however need to be conscious of how they come over and, if body language can assist their cause, they would be sensible to use it. Negotiators would normally want to appear open, confident, engaged and enthusiastic. Set out below is a matrix which gives examples of positive and negative behaviours said to be associated with these attributes.

How you look

	Positive Behaviours	Negative Behaviours
Open and Relaxed / Defensive or Nervous	Arms extended away from your body. Open hands. Relaxed body posture. Unbuttoned collar. Removing coat or jacket. Eyes wide open. Slight smile.	Crossed arms. Tightly clenched hands. Hand partially covering the mouth. Nose rubbing. Mouth pursed Rigid or slumped body posture. Head downturned.

Confident / Overconfident	Head up. Relaxed but upright body posture. Open hands. Sit with whole body facing the person who is speaking.	Leaning back, one leg resting across the other knee, with both hands behind the head. Sitting with one leg dangling over one arm of the chair. Standing with hands clasped behind back.
Engaged / Uncertain or Suspicious	Sitting on the edge of the chair and leaning slightly forward. Uncrossing arms and legs. Moving closer. Good eye contact. Mirroring the facial expressions, head movements and posture of the person who is speaking.	Rubbing your ear. Sideways glances Minimal or no eye contact Turning the body away from the speaker Fiddling with glasses, pen, etc. Fidgeting Looking over the top of your glasses. Tapping fingers.
Interested/ Bored or Impatient	Tilting head. Putting your hand to your cheek. Stroking your chin.	Drumming of fingers. Cupping the head in the palm of the hand. Legs crossed and foot swinging. Brushing clothes. Looking at your watch or the exit.

Fig. 4

And how you sound

Then there is your voice; not all of us are born with an engaging way of speaking, but it is something that can be learned and practiced.

A good public speaker will have clear diction; vary the volume (to stress particular points); use tone to reinforce the words as appropriate; and change their speed of delivery, pausing occasionally for added effect. The pitch should generally be lower rather than higher, as this gives the voice authority, but this must be varied to add variety.

A lively and well-modulated voice will show you to be a relaxed, enthusiastic person (even if you are neither of these things!). By comparison, speaking too rapidly, with a pitch that rises at the end of a sentence, can sound nervous and uncertain. Many of us speak too quickly when under pressure and pauses seem far longer to the speaker than the listener. Equally off-putting is a flat, monotone speech pattern which will inevitably come over as uninspiring and boring.

It can be a shock to hear a recording your own speaking voice (it still is for me) but use it as a learning opportunity. You may find you have picked up some mannerisms which can be irritating to a listener. Do you slur sometimes, mumble or repeat certain phrases? If you do, listeners may be straining to catch your meaning and, unintentionally, you will be annoying your audience.

Experienced negotiators know how to vary their delivery to suit the phase of the negotiation. For example, they will start informal and relaxed; become more crisp and business-like when the hard bargaining gets underway, only to relax the tone and pace again as the deal is reached and the discussions become more collaborative.

And what you say

The language of collective bargaining is cursed by gobbledygook. In what context, other than the bargaining table, would you use the expression 'derisory', as in "management's offer is derisory"? Such hackneyed jargon only serves to irritate.

For example, what does "our fair and reasonable offer" mean, apart from "we like it"? It has no descriptive power, but is guaranteed to prompt a response from the other side to the effect that, in their eyes, it is neither fair, nor indeed reasonable.

Similarly, avoid using leading questions. Although often asked inadvertently and possibly with the best of intentions, they offend because, to the receiver, they are patronising and implicitly judgemental. Classic include: "I'm sure you can see the advantages of this, can't you?" and "Don't you think that would be a good idea?" "As I'm sure you would agree" is similarly counterproductive and almost guaranteed to elicit a "No" response.

Another much overused phrase is "I hear what you say"; this is almost invariably followed by the qualifying word "but", which thereby renders the rest of the statement valueless. The true meaning of this piece of bargaining jargon is usually, "I have heard the words you have used but I have instantly dismissed their content".

But, without doubt, my personal un-favourite, is "with all due respect": an expression which generally means precisely the opposite of a dictionary definition of the words it comprises!

So, unless your intent is to irritate, watch what you say. The words you use can annoy your opponent as much as how you say them.

A note of caution

I have already expressed a degree of scepticism. I now want to add a note of caution. First impressions make a big impact, but they can be wrong, so don't jump to conclusions.

Body language can be deceptive. It is far from being a foolproof diagnostic for two reasons: firstly, individuals have their own mannerisms which, unintentionally, can send out erroneous messages. Someone who rubs their nose may have an itch, and not be defensive or nervous at all. Secondly, body language can be used to disguise emotions and deliberately send out false signals. Either way, don't jump to conclusions. Always use questioning to confirm your analysis and be ready to change your views.

There are exceptions to all this. One or two negotiators cultivate their individuality. Their dress, manner of speaking and choice of language are well outside usual business practice. But these tend to be forceful characters with extrovert personalities, and this approach works for them because it adds to their impact. As ever, make your choice knowingly.

Smiling & using humour

Remember to smile. A smile can be a useful technique because it lends itself to a number of different situations. You can use it to draw attention and provoke a response. The other side will want to know what is amusing you. A smile and a nod is not only a good way of showing you are paying attention but, used appropriately, it can build trust, encourage openness and diffuse tension.

But smile, don't grin, and don't overdo it over you risk the "you're not taking this seriously reaction", so smile at the right time. Jokes similarly can backfire and are best avoided, but an appropriate, well timed light-hearted comment can lower the tension and build rapport.

A self-deprecating, amusing remark is fine, but humour at the expense of others is risky. Avoid any humour that could be misinterpreted, including anything that could be deliberately misinterpreted. Words cannot be unsaid, so if you are caught making an inappropriate remark, the other side will pick on it, seize the moral high ground and use it against you. You will live to regret it.

Getting started

Before getting down to business, it is customary to open with informal pleasantries. It can be surprising to a newcomer to negotiations just how warm these initial contacts can be. It can be useful to be able to offer refreshments at this point. Commonly, the individuals on both sides of the table will know each other well and able to engage in a degree of good natured conversation. But don't be deceived, the tone can change quickly. Because both sides know each other, introductions are often skipped no doubt because they seem superfluous. However, this misses an opportunity. Introducing colleagues by name (using both first name and surname) shows respect to your opponents; marks the opening of the meeting with appropriate formality; and provides a convenient way to present your team to the other side, underlining their roles and status in the organisation.

You should now seize the initiative but without making it too obvious. As lead negotiator you want to be the chair of the meeting. To do this you need to act more like a judge than an adversary, so use the opportunity to provide an overview of the situation outlining, in neutral terms, the events leading up to the meeting.

Remember, right from the outset, they will be scrutinising your demeanour, picking up on your enthusiasm, assessing your sincerity, and reacting to the tone and pace of your delivery. You need to demonstrate therefore that you are here to do business. So how you act should be designed to persuade them that they can rely on your integrity, knowledge and expertise and, above all, show that they can trust you to deliver what is agreed. If you can get the other side to relax from the outset, your task will be so much easier. It is well worth therefore practicing in advance your introductory remarks. Then, having established yourself as the de facto chair, invite the other side to present their case.

Any meeting needs an agreed agenda (implicit or explicit) listing the subjects for consideration but, in negotiations, it cannot be too rigid as the discussions must be allowed to flow to encourage new ideas and options to emerge.

Setting the agenda

In employee relations, it is common practice for the Union to have presented its claim or grievances in writing before the talks begin. For this reason the Union's claim is often used as an agenda for the negotiations and they therefore 'go first'. However, good employer negotiators are not content to be reactive and play the rules set by the other side.

Rather than accepting the union's initial list for discussion, experienced negotiators will seek to add new items; agree to discuss a union's agenda item provided only if it is linked to one of theirs; or, remove something from their shopping list in exchange for a similar concession by the other side. This continues throughout the negotiations until the outline shape of a deal becomes clear.

A common example of this would be where management

responds to a claim for increased holiday entitlement by insisting that this be linked to concessions on tighter controls of uncertificated absence. Deals with 'strings' attached generally will not be popular with the other side, but such proposals may open up areas for fruitful negotiation and mutual benefit.

Case Study 4

A few years ago I conciliated in a pay dispute in a transport company. The union were seeking an above inflation pay increase as part of their campaign to 'catch up' with similar workers in the locality. The employer negotiators argued that the company could not afford this, as they themselves were tied into long term contract which only provided for cost of living increases. Indeed, the company was already running at a loss and its future was uncertain. Negotiations became acrimonious and a ballot for industrial action gave the Union a clear mandate for industrial action.

In conciliation, management responded by tabling a raft of proposals aimed at increasing productivity, which they claimed would ensure the company's survival, and fund a higher than average pay increase; all of which the Union saw as unacceptable. After lengthy talks, both sides agreed to withdraw their respective claims. Settlement for that year was at the level of the retail price index. Management did not get its productivity increase and the workforce did not have an inflation-plus pay increase. Although this could be regarded as lose-lose, nevertheless, it did avert a strike (which would have been very damaging to the company and possibly spread to other sites).

Having made a positive impression and got the negotiations off to a good start, your job is now to sit back and listen – and that is not as easy as it sounds.

Listening & observing

"Listening is not waiting to talk."
Scott Ginsberg

Negotiators need to cultivate the technique of positive listening. At this stage you should listen politely, nodding and smiling at appropriate moments. This does not mean you agree, but it does show you are listening and have an open mind. Do not attack their views at this stage but show you understand what they are saying and why they feel as they do. The other side should feel that you are treating them with respect and giving them a fair opportunity to state their case.

Positive listening means listening to what is said, but it also means watching how it is said, as well as spotting what is not being said. Positive listening includes noting the body language of their lead negotiator, and seeing how the other side's team members unintentionally respond to what is being said on their behalf. Are their clues here to their intentions? Are they sending out signals, deliberate or unintentional? We shall return to 'signalling' later.

Positive listening can be a difficult art to master. It is tiring, especially if you think you have heard all of what is being said before. But don't make assumptions. If you start getting judgemental you will stop listening. So get curious. It requires concentration, practice and, above all, self-control. All too often we are not truly listening, we are reacting. We have picked up only a small part of what is being communicated because we have stopped listening and are already planning our reply. We don't like what we are hearing and we want to talk, not listen. But if we focus on listening, we may well learn something to our advantage. Then, if we time our intervention and base it on a fuller understanding of the other side's interests, we might well be in a stronger position.

You may dislike what is being said, but your silence doesn't mean assent. You can listen calmly and attentively, giving non-verbal indications of interest. You can nod, smile encouragingly, maintain eye contact, and then be seen to make a note, thereby emphasising that you recognise that a salient point has been made. None of this implies that you agree with what is being said, but it does show that you are listening. Other techniques can support this approach. For example, feeding back a précis of what you have been told, using expressions like: "Have I got this right? Are you saying...?

As we have already noted, summarising has a variety of uses, but here it is showing that you are paying attention and showing the other side proper respect. At this point, non-controversial questions to clarify a point of detail similarly can be used to put the other side at their ease. As a result, they may then communicate more than they intended. Now, when you pick your moment to disagree, your response will have more impact, as it will come over as considered and judicial, rather than immediate and partial.

Managing expectations

The opening presentation is your opportunity to get some of your ideas in the heads of the opposing team. Perhaps even more importantly, this is your chance stop them becoming committed to unachievable ambitions at this early stage. The negotiations will be at risk becoming protracted and excessively adversarial if the other side persist in holding out for options that you cannot live with. Your presentation should therefore not only convey your ideas but also make a start on managing, and lowering, their expectations.

Mistakenly, employers at this point often fall into the trap of making a lengthy presentation. The reality is however that the attention span of the other side will be very short, so it is sensible to keep the initial response brief and use the time effectively. When preparing your opening presentation, it is useful to remember the old trainers' dictum "tell them what you will tell them; tell them; and, then tell them what you've told them."

The response should start with an explanation of your key arguments and facts. Resist the urge to give too many arguments at this stage; the impact will be lessened, and the other side will only pick off the weaker ones and feel they have thereby gained an advantage (you will no doubt seek to do the same to them). You should then lead in to the substance of your reply. Opinions vary, but this way round you are more likely to keep the other side's negotiators listening. The danger is that, faced by the substance of your opening position, they will stop listening and not take on board your main underpinning arguments. Better therefore to lead them through the key arguments before stating the detail of your opening response.

You will have prepared your opening presentation in advance, but be ready to adapt it to reflect what you have now heard. This will show the other side that you have showed them respect, you have listened to what they have said and responded accordingly. But, remember, this is not a debate, it is a negotiation, and you won't win prizes for scoring debating points; indeed, this will only irritate and encourage opponents to become more intractable. By all means challenge their assertions, identify inconsistencies in their reasoning and question their conclusions, but do so in a positive manner, with the aim of getting their agreement not of showing your superiority.

Always bear in mind that their values may not be your values: your case will have a far greater impact if you are able to couch it in their terms. For example, if they have stressed the need for fairness, explain why your deal is fair and return to this theme throughout the presentation. And don't forget to explain your values to them, thereby helping them understand why you have adopted the positions you have. Finally, emphasise the benefits to them of reaching a settlement.

Negotiators are not dispassionate. The outcome of the talks may have serious consequences both for the negotiators and for the people they represent; so showing emotion is not necessarily a bad thing. Good negotiators need to show that they care and be able to do this convincingly. Without 'emotional intelligence' negotiators won't be able to understand the intensity that collective bargaining can provoke. But they must do this without losing their composure or their self-awareness.

As Jean Giraudoux, the French diplomat, dramatist and novelist, said:

> "The secret of success is sincerity. Once you can fake that you've got it made."

Having kept their attention, invite questions, offer to clarify any points and encourage a dialogue, showing that you are ready to be flexible and are prepared to discuss the issues in a constructive manner. At this stage you may wish to have members of your team primed to give short presentations on points of detail. In this way you have not shut down the negotiations through a blank rebuttal of their claim (which in itself can lead to an early breakdown) and have kept the talks relaxed but business-like.

Questioning & probing

"I keep six honest serving men: They taught me all I knew: Their names are What and Why and When and How and Where and Who."
Rudyard Kipling

Having established your respective positions, and the main arguments that underpin them, the next step is to find out more about the points on which they may be prepared to move. By use of probing questions you should seek to identify the weaknesses and the strengths of their position. Research in the late 1970s by Neil Rackham and John Carlisle found that skilled negotiators ask twice as many questions as average negotiators.

Negotiating is about mutual discovery of your respective positions. The art of negotiating is in the pace and extent of this disclosure. In traditional, adversarial bargaining the aim is for you to disclose less and find out more than they do. But, a word of warning, if the other side feel the exchange is all one-way, they will respond negatively.

Effective questioning techniques are therefore central to the process. You want to find out what their bottom-line positions are on the matters under negotiation. But more than that, you want to discover what their interests and concerns are that underpin these positions. This way you can try and package your response and put it in language that suits their needs and values.

Fisher & Ury say that *"statements generate resistance, whereas questions generate answers... Questions do not criticise, they educate."*

Well, maybe! It very much depends on the questions and how they are asked. Rhetorical or loaded questions can actually increase tension, for example: "when are you going to stop driving this company into bankruptcy?"

It has also been suggested that you should never ask a question if you know you are not going to be able to live with the answer. There may be questions that don't need to be asked at this stage in the negotiations. It may be that the answers would be damaging and are best left unsaid, at least for now. But, generally, you will need to get positions out into the open before progress can be made and questioning can achieve this. As ever, it is a judgement call.

As Rudyard Kipling knew, asking questions is how we learn. Thought to have originated at Toyota, the technique called the '7 Whys' (or sometimes '6 Whys') was developed as part of the company's manufacturing quality improvement programme. It can be a powerful way of getting below the surface and getting the real answer. To practice this, don't accept a response to a question as being the true answer. Press on and question the answers you are given seven times. The theory is that, by asking 'why' seven times, you get to successive levels of underlying detail until, at the seventh time of asking, you get to the root cause of any problem.

However, a word of caution: people don't react well to an inquisition because they feel they are being dominated. Handled badly, this type of persistent questioning will seem aggressive. Your questions should come over as an honest attempt to establish the facts, not feel like an interrogation, so a lighter touch may be needed. The other side will clam up if they feel threatened, but they are far more likely to give something away if they are allowed to relax and get into a two-way discourse. A good place to begin is with easy to answer, non-controversial questions which should open up the proceedings, because without interaction, no progress can be made. So start by asking straightforward questions like: "are you asking for the percentage increase to apply equally across all grades of staff?"

Then move on to open questions (that is questions that can't easily be answered by a terse 'yes' or 'no'). The aim here is to get a dialogue going, so use questions like: "what are your concerns here?", "how do you think we should take this forward?", and "what are your priorities here?" Questioning like this can defuse conflict and open up a constructive dialogue and are particularly useful in the early phases of a negotiation. They can also be used in response to what you perceive as a signal from the other side (we will come to signalling shortly). For example: "you say you still can't agree to our offer, so what do you see as the main sticking points preventing agreement." This should get them to open up, but don't expect necessarily to like what you hear!

This is not to say that there is no place for direct, pointed questioning in negotiations, or even for asking closed questions, quite the contrary, but they need to be used knowingly, sparingly and at the right time. Direct questions are best used to probe the other side's position and get to their underlying interests and concerns. Good questioning can avoid misunderstandings and check understanding. To do this, use reflective questions link to summarising. For example: "have I got this right, are you saying...?" If you find that you still don't understand, find out. Ask questions like: "can you expand on that a bit?" "Could you tell me more about that?" "Why is that particularly important to you?" You can even ask about their feelings; but this line of questioning is best left until you feel that sufficient rapport has been established for them to open up and discuss with you the underlying values and beliefs. Nevertheless, such values underpin the positions they are adopting, so a genuine discussion at this level can enhance your prospect of securing a deal because it could allow you to recast your offer in terms they will feel easier to accept.

But beware, even experienced negotiators fall into the trap of making assumptions about the other side's position, usually assuming the worst! So, if there is any room for doubt, use questioning to check understanding and agreement before moving on. This becomes particularly important as the negotiation progresses towards its final stage, there will come a time when you will need to pin down the detail of the option being discussed. For example: "OK, would you move the settlement date if that helped us offer a bigger percentage pay increase?" It is also sensible to avoid multiple questions, that is asking more than one questions in one go. For example, "...so would you prefer a phased pay increase in years one and two to a lower settlement in one year; a deal on the bonus or underpinning to protect the lower paid?" This tends to provoke answers that are even more confusing than the question. When you can, keep it simple.

Despite your neutral questioning, you may well encounter hostility to your opening moves. A good aphorism to remember at this point is "don't get mad, get curious." What is provoking this behaviour; has something happened? A particularly a good question at this point (appropriately framed) is "why now?" You need to know why they are now pursuing this issue so strongly. Of course, you may think you already know the answer, but beware making assumptions and check using neutral questioning. For example: "I can see you feel strongly about this, can you explain your view of the problem?"

You may also find a reluctance to respond to a particular line of questioning. If the other side avoid answering on particular a point, get curious but don't pounce! Rephrase the question and attack it from another angle. If this doesn't work make a note and move on, but be sure to return to it later. If they still are evasive, consider moving to more direct questions and evaluate their response.

Having used questioning to establish the issues and what lies behind them, the next step will be to start generating possible solutions. The feel of the negotiations should now change, with a move away from the formal exchange of opening positions, to a more open flow of questioning and counter-questioning. As you move towards this next stage, hypothetical questions involving phrases like "supposing...would you consider...?", and "if you..., then perhaps we..." start being used to encourage option generation.

As progress is made, the language should then sharpen up, with more specific questions such as: "if we..., then would you...?" being asked. We are now close to reaching hard bargaining, so closed questions will be necessary to check details of offers and counter-offers. This technique is returned to in the next chapter.

The art of questioning is more than the words used. The manner in which questions are asked, and the body language used, can make difficult questions seem less threatening and so elicit the information you are seeking. If you can smile, appear supportive and non-threatening, and then ask a carefully crafted, probing question that makes them stop and think, then you are on the top of your game.

Of course, as well as asking questions you will need to reply to the other side's questions. How you respond will say a lot about you as a negotiator. If you come over as open and honest, your image will be enhanced. If you appear evasive or reluctant to share information the other side will conclude that you have something to hide. Even if it appears hostile or negative, treat their questioning as a positive sign; it means that a dialogue has been established and it provides an opportunity for you to develop your case.

And listen before you reply. This may seem obvious but in fact negotiators can be concentrating so hard on what they are about to say that they forget to listen to what is being said to them. If you do this, you will miss not only what is being said but what is not being said – the signals being given by the other side. As we shall now see, signalling is a key skill for negotiators

Signalling

Having made your initial presentation and probed their position through questioning, you need to start exploring areas for possible movement. But, you don't want to give too much away, and nor will they. So, how do you indicate areas where a trade of concessions may be productive, and how do they tell you the same, without revealing too much, too quickly? The answer is signalling.

Signalling is the use of hints and cues to prompt reactions in the other side without explicitly saying what you mean. It may seem circuitous, but it is the key to effective negotiating, and it works. You must be able to send signals and be alert to receiving them.

The complication with signals is that the message given by a combination of verbal and non-verbal communication can be contradictory. This dissonance can be intentional, intended to communicate a deliberate mixed message, or it may be unintentional, letting slip more than was intended.

The classic signal qualifies what is being said. For example, "The deal is completely unacceptable in its present form." The 'weasel words' here are "in its present form". What the negotiator is saying is that their team's mandate is to reject the offer, but, if it were reformulated, then the answer might be yes. Other examples include: "we just can't do this now", suggesting perhaps that the time may not be right but may be at some undisclosed point in the future; "it is disgraceful that you are disregarding the financial hardship that this will cause our members," which might mean that compensation could change their minds; or, "we would never sell jobs in this way," leaving the question hanging, in what way would they allow jobs to go?

So why doesn't the negotiator simply say what they need to make a deal acceptable? To do this would appear as weakness, both to those on their side of the table and to their constituents outside the room. To a careful listener however such a response provides an opening that, with time and careful questioning, can move the negotiations forward. A good negotiator can communicate possible areas for fruitful discussion; concerns they have that will need to be addressed if agreement is to be reached; and, points on which, if pressed, concessions could be made.

It is of course more difficult if a negotiator doesn't know that they are giving out signals and this won't always be apparent. The response however should always be the same: listen intently, pause, question carefully, and then respond cautiously, often with intentional signals of your own. If you make a mistake, and it is easily done, admit it, apologise, take a step back and start again. The real mistake would be to try and cover up an error by using implausible arguments or by adopting untenable positions.

The negotiations are now well underway. You have 'set out your stall' and, by the effective use of questioning, probing and signalling allows negotiators you have begun to narrow the differences. You should by now be able start to identify areas for compromise. Now the hard work really begins.

5

MIDDLE GAME

"Honest disagreement is often a good sign of progress."
Mahatma Gandhi

This chapter will help negotiators start to make proposals to the other side and get into the business of hard bargaining. It will suggest techniques to help them achieve this and respond when the pressure is on.

Movement

"Benefits should be conferred gradually; and in that way they will taste better."
Niccolo Machiavelli

In almost all negotiations, both sides will need to be prepared to move from their opening positions if agreement is to be reached. But how they move will say a lot about them as negotiators and, potentially, reveal much about the strength of their case. I think it no exaggeration to say that knowing when and how to move is the key skill for a negotiator.

There has been little empirical research on the effectiveness of negotiating practices in the workplace. However, during the 1970s and 1980s, John Carlisle worked with the Huthwaite Research Group looking at negotiation and selling skills. They observed thousands of negotiations but when they watched 'good' negotiators they noticed several distinguishing features in their behaviour. Carlisle, together with his colleague, Neil Rackham, produced their conclusions, one of the most interesting of which was that skilled negotiators made immediate counter-proposals much less frequently than average negotiators.

(A summary of the Huthwaite findings can be found at: *www. salesskills.co.uk/pdf/whitepapers/NEGS-developing_effective_ negotiation_skills.pdf*)

Why should this be? I believe it is because the art of negotiating is to get the other side to move, not you. With this in mind, be cautious about responding too quickly to any proposal they make. This may sound counter-intuitive; surely negotiation is about option generation so why not produce lots of alternatives to help resolve an issue? The problem is that to do this too early can actually hinder progress. It is easy to get sidetracked in a negotiation and, if you introduce too many new alternatives too quickly you can confuse the picture. You need first to deal with their proposal, indeed they will resent being asked to move on until this is done. If you try you risk being seen as obstructive and not taking their proposal seriously.

So when the other side responds by making a proposal, do not respond immediately with a counter-proposal. Instead, explain why their proposal is impractical or unacceptable to you; return to your position, restate it; then use questioning to get behind their objections.

When you do move (and at some point you almost certainly will have to) always have a good reason for so doing. It will enhance perceptions of your integrity as a negotiator if you are able to give good, convincing reasons for making a concession. For example, you could say something to the effect that "we have listened carefully to what you have said and, if it would be helpful to you, we would be prepared to..." In particular, it should never appear as though you are moving your position in response to a threat. If you do, you encourage them to use this tactic again.

Once an offer is on the table, it is hard to take it back: words, once said, cannot be unsaid, so concessions must not be made lightly. One offer often leads to another offer; so, once you start moving, it can be hard to stop moving. The trick therefore is always to get them to move as well. The traditional view is that you should never give "owt for nowt", never give something for nothing. Always trade concessions and, when you make a concession, you should do so with apparent reluctance, playing down the value of their concession to you. The aim should always be to trade what is cheap for you for what is valuable to them.

Movement needs to be made, but it should be slow, irregular, and made for a purpose. It should be slow, with concessions made reluctantly, because the other side need to feel that they have earned it. As Thomas Paine, the 18th century writer and political pamphleteer, said: *"What we obtain too cheap, we esteem too lightly."* So, if you have made the other side work hard for a concession, they will value it and be more likely to be willing to exchange it for something you want.

Movement should be irregular, because you do not want to be seen to be predictable. Movement must be made with a purpose; it should gain you a specific benefit. Making concessions has been described as "parachute negotiating"; you start high up and descend slowly. All well and good, but make sure you don't plummet! Your opening position can be high, but it must be credible, and it needs to be a controlled descent.

So if an agreement is to be reached without protracted conflict and damage to the relationship, the negotiations must be interactive; there must be 'give and take'. But, who is giving and who is taking? Who is making the concessions and who is refusing to move their position significantly? Try and look at this as objectively as you can, but you will be partisan. In my experience, negotiators always think that it is they are doing all the giving, and the other side that is doing all the taking.

Behaviour labelling

Most of the findings of Rackham and Carlisle reinforced what was already widely regarded as good practice, although it was good to have it confirmed. One exception was 'Behaviour Labelling', which I had not heard of before. Huthwaites used it to describe the practice of good negotiators who give advance indication of what they are about to say. The example they gave was, instead of just asking "How many units are there?" good negotiators are more likely to say "Can

I ask a question – how many units are there?" Instead of making a proposal, they began "If I could make a suggestion........"

At first sight this may seem like over-politeness, but on reflection I have come to appreciate its utility, because labelling serves to get the listeners' attention. What is more, it creates a pause by announcing the intention in advance, and its respectful nature encourages an equally polite response. I started using it, and it worked. In fact, when I said "can I ask a question?", I then waited for them to say "yes", before asking my question. This seems to underline the technique and nobody ever said "no, you can't"!

Huthwaites gave one caveat; don't label disagreement. Skilled negotiators are more likely to begin with the reasons for disagreeing and lead up to the disagreement. Again, I quite agree.

Option generation

As we have seen, option generation shouldn't be done too early, but if the negotiations are going well, the questioning should now start to take the form of "what ifs". The use of hypothetical questions allows negotiators to explore options which go beyond their original position and start to identify the shape the eventual deal will take. To an experienced negotiator, the sound of the words "if we ... then would you" means that a dialogue is being established. However, a degree of caution is necessary: such questions must be couched in strictly non-committal language. No negotiator wants to sound too eager or move too quickly and there is still a long way to go. However, using words like "what if...then perhaps" allow ideas to be floated and lets the other side respond in similar terms. You are now exploring possibilities without yet making formal offers which can be difficult to withdraw later.

How you describe an option will greatly influence its acceptability, so if you can use their language and values and build in reassurances, so much the better. The other side will always be suspicious, so it helps if you can get them to contribute to the development of an option. Therefore, don't present them with a completely worked idea (though have the details in your back pocket): be prepared to move on the details but not the underlying principles.

Persuasion

Most negotiators concentrate on the logic of their case and build rational arguments to support it. However, whilst your approach must be rational, you shouldn't ignore the awkward fact that negotiators, and their constituents, commit emotionally to the positions they adopt, which are underpinned not just by their interests but also the values they hold. It is therefore a valid part of persuasion to appeal to the emotions. To do this, your words must speak to the values of your opponent; as Nelson Mandela put it, *"If you talk to a man in a language he understands, that goes to his head. If you talk to him in his language, that goes to his heart."*

Persuasion is not so much getting the other side to see things your way; rather, it is getting them to accept that what you are saying has benefits to them and is the best that they can get. So, get them to see what is in it for them, where possible by using their language and values, but do so without appearing patronising. Show your appreciation when they make a concession, however small it may be. Always minimise the benefits of your proposal to you and never, ever give any indication that, by agreeing, they are losing and you are winning. Indeed, if they come away thinking that it is their side that is ahead of the game, so much the better.

Remember, the benefit you are offering can be of greater value to them than it is a cost to you. For example, I have helped draw up many conciliation agreements in settlement of employment tribunal claims. Normally these would focus on sums of money, but not always: I have done deals which included the retention of fitted carpets, a pet snake and ownership of a guard dog! When dealing with dismissed sales reps, the issue was often retention of the company car. In such cases, keeping the car on the dismissed employee's driveway meant far more to the individual than the actual second hand value of the vehicle.

Finally, to be persuasive an argument must not only convey benefits but it must also provide reassurances to counter their fears. So play to their needs and assuage their fears.

For example: "a three year pay deal will give your members the security of knowing that their pay is going to increase year on year, and will increase the base figure for overtime and shift premiums. I understand your concerns about the third year so, if it makes it easier for you, we could consider building in an underpinning of RPI in year three." Both sides can benefit from a three year pay deal: the employer gains from being able to make better financial planning; the employees benefits from the certainty of knowing they will get pay increases. But, the Union negotiators will be reluctant to agree because inflation could increase, making what looks a good deal now, much poorer in two years time. Underpinning in year three could go some way to making the deal acceptable.

So, what is the difference between a persuasive negotiator and a manipulative negotiator? The answer is that you will willingly go along with a persuasive person, but react badly if you feel you are being manipulated. The difference then is that to be persuasive you must honest and credible – or at least appear so!

Saying No

Of course, the other side are likely to come up with proposals you cannot live with. If you reject them out of hand, this will be perceived as negative, indeed all they will hear is 'no'. Ideally, you should never say no, rather you should respond by building on what they say, explaining why your proposal meets their concerns.

However, in reality, this will not always be possible. There will be times when a line of thinking they are taking has to be closed down or it will raise their expectations unrealistically. But only say no when you mean it and when you have to. In these, hopefully, rare circumstances, first be at pains to say why you can't accept, explaining both your reasons and your needs.

Do this by trying to say 'no' positively. William Ury has devoted an entire book to this very point and it is well worth a read. In *The Power of a Positive No* he describes a three-stage process of *Yes! No. Yes?* His thesis is that *"the first Yes expresses your interests, the No asserts your **power**, and the second Yes furthers your **relationship**."*

My experience is very similar. Good negotiators always outline, in neutral language, the problems they have with the other side's proposals before actually saying 'no'. What they are doing here is trying to bring the other side with them, explaining in advance their reasons, before stating their rejection. If you do it the other way round, and preface your reasons with a blunt 'no', the likelihood is that the other side will stop listening. Don't close down the negotiations but make a positive out of the negative, perhaps by signalling an area for possible movement. You want to encourage them to come back with revised proposals that may be closer to meeting your concerns, so help them do so without them losing face.

Summarising

Summarising is a key skill, much used by expert negotiators because, when done well, it can be used to serve a number of functions throughout the various stages of a negotiation.

Summarising can be used as a way of steering the direction of the talks and, thereby, assuming control of the negotiations. If you can be first one to summarise where you have reached in a negotiation you will be setting and controlling the agenda. By doing this you have taken the initiative and, in effect, will be chairing the meeting.

In addition, summarising is an effective form of positive listening which builds up rapport in a negotiation. It doesn't mean that you necessarily are agreeing with what has been said to you; but it does show that you are paying attention, showing the other side proper respect and taking what they have to say seriously.

After a period of "what if" exchanges, summarising will clarify exactly what is being floated and what the conditions attached to any such arrangement would look like. Summarising therefore stops mistakes being made. Negotiations can become highly complex and emotionally charged. It is easy to make an error by misunderstanding a point and, as a result, adopting a position from which it is difficult and embarrassing to pull back.

Summarising is a useful way of pausing without appearing obstructive and can be used to review progress made so far, emphasising what has been achieved without ignoring what still has to be done. This can be a precursor to an adjournment which will allow one, or both sides, to reflect on what has been said and consider their next moves. By confirming the progress made so far, you are recording what has been achieved before moving on to the next point. However, because everything has a cost and all items will be inter-related, it will be hard to confirm agreement on one point until the whole package has been gone through. If this becomes of concern to you, one useful tactic is to seek provisional agreement, making it clear that is subject to progress being made on the other subjects for discussion.

Summarising can even be used aggressively, by mirroring back what has been said to you, with the aim of putting doubt in the minds of the other side. This is delivered by saying something like: "what you are really saying is…" followed by a rhetorical question, like "do you honestly think that is practical?"

But, for whatever purpose you employ summarising, it is essential that you summarise accurately as a mistake is likely to be regarded either as incompetence on your part or, equally uncharitably, as a deliberate underhand manoeuvre. Inaccurate summarising can even be used deliberately as we shall see in the chapter on Dirty Tricks.

As well as summarising yourself, get the other side to summarise. You can do this by asking them to restate their position to help you understand. This carries with it all the benefits of summarising, but gets them to do the work and take ownership of what is said.

Adjournments

As already noted, in traditional bargaining, negotiations are often little more than a dialogue between lead negotiators of either side. Adjournments allow all concerned to step back and reflect on where the talks have reached. It never pays to be rushed into a making a decision and adjournments will give you time to pause and examine a new option. But adjournments can serve a variety of other purposes:

- They allow team members to speak. They may be desperate to share their views and vent their feelings. It is very frustrating to remain silent when things aren't going your way, especially if you feel sidelined by the process.
- Adjournments can be used to defuse tension or prevent walkouts. It is a fact that, after well-timed break, negotiators

will have calmed down and are more likely to look at matters afresh.

- On occasions, one of your side may let the pressure get to them. This may take the form of aggression or other unprofessional behaviour. By calling an adjournment this will give you time to quieten them down and reassert team discipline.
- A point may come up which is outside your brief. You may need to talk to someone outside of your negotiating team. Adjournments can give you time to consult quickly with constituents or experts.
- As a team member you may even feel that your lead negotiator straying too far from the mandate. An adjournment will give you the opportunity to get them back on track.

But, like all tactics, if overdone adjournments can be counterproductive. Overuse of adjournments interrupts the flow of negotiations and prevents a dialogue being developed. Adjournments can therefore even be used to deliberately provoke a walkout.

If one side responds to every initiative by calling for adjournment it will frustrate the negotiations and suggest that, not only do they distrust the other side, but they do not have confidence in their own lead negotiator. As a conciliator, some of the most difficult negotiations I have been involved in were little more than an exchange of offers and counter-offer (with little questioning or probing), interspersed by adjournments. This so inhibited debate so that little progress could be made and the negotiations became protracted and ill-tempered.

Secondly, over-lengthy or open-ended adjournments can have a negative effect on negotiations. I confess that this is a mistake I have made. As a conciliator, I often need to talk to one side separately and I would call for a quick five minutes adjournment. Despite being well aware of the need to maintain the pace and impetus of a negotiation, my quick five minutes have been known to last for a lot longer.

As a rule of thumb, adjournments should last no longer than half an hour. If longer is needed it is best to arrange these to coincide with a meal break. Repeated, lengthy adjournments risk being seen as deliberate time wasting and likely to provoke a hostile response. I can recall one that lasted over a day – you can imagine the reaction this provoked from the other side!

One way of avoiding the negative aspects of adjournments lies in how you present your ideas. If you table a complex set of proposals, requiring detailed examination and careful reading, then the other side will need a lengthy side meeting to put together their response. If you need to do this (and cannot provide it in writing in advance of the meeting) a better way may be to call a halt to proceedings and agree to meet again, if possible later that week. However, you may be working to a tight deadline so, if necessary, be prepared to sit and wait.

Threats, coercion and the application of pressure

"War is just when it is necessary; arms are permissible when there is no hope except in arms."
Niccolo Machiavelli

"I do not hold that we should rearm in order to fight. I hold that we should rearm in order to parley."
Winston Churchill

"Negotiations are a euphemism for capitulation if the shadow of power is not cast across the bargaining table."
George Pratt Schultz

When I have run training courses on negotiating, some participants have been shocked by my suggestion that threats have a role to play in bargaining. But, just as *"war is an extension of politics by other means"*, as the Prussian military philosopher, Carl von Clausewitz, famously said, so industrial action (and management imposition) is an extension of collective bargaining. Coercion and the threat of coercive action is part of negotiation, albeit sometimes unspoken.

Whether it is a call for an industrial action ballot, or an announcement by management of their intention to impose a change in working practices, it is there because it is a reflection of the perceived balance of power that underlies the negotiating relationship.

In employment relations negotiations the power balance is based on the damage which each can cause the other if they do not concede. Usually, however, both sides suffer as a consequence of the exercise of power. The employer can lose business, customers, profits and reputational damage. Employees lose wages when they are on strike and, should lasting damage be done to the company, they may even lose their jobs. For this reason, it is often said that coercion will result in lose-lose. But this is not always the case.

Case Study 5

I conciliated in a collective dispute at an airport catering company. The Union was threatening industrial action in pursuit of a substantial pay increase. Management responded by saying that a strike could close the company.

The Union called their bluff. The response was that even if the company shut down as a consequence, another catering company would come in to pick up the contract and their drivers would move to the new operator.

Privately, the employer acknowledged to me that this had some truth to it. A fact that substantially affected the power balance and enhanced the Union's negotiating position.

Threats have their uses; they may sound negative but they can be a timely reminder of the likely consequences of the other side's proposed course of action. If you have a credible alternative to reaching agreement, then pointing this out can considerably strengthen your position, but expect it to be received as a threat. The effectiveness of threats will depend on how they are delivered and how they are perceived. But threats are only worth making if you have the capacity to deliver and are prepared to act on them. Otherwise, they risk being seen as empty bluffs and your credibility will be at risk. You can end up being painted into a corner and forced to implement the coercive action you had only intended as a threat.

How to threaten

A threat can simply be a timely reminder of the consequences of not reaching agreement: "We both know what will happen if we can't get a deal." Or it can be overt: "If we don't do a deal today, there will be redundancies/I will ballot for industrial action." In other words a threat can be a warning of imminent danger; or, if put more strongly, it can be declaration of an intention to take coercive action.

The trick in negotiation is knowing both when to do it and how to do it. When are arguments, however well made, inadequate? When should you raise the stakes and threaten coercion? Made at the wrong time, threats will be counterproductive. The parties can fall into a spiral of threat and counter-threat, escalating levels of conflict and entrenching positions, setting back any prospect of a negotiated settlement. The other side may well conclude that, as breakdown is inevitable, they should concentrate on making preparations to live with the consequences by preparing their "walk-away alternative".

It is also possible to make a threat without intending to do so. For example, introducing a deadline can easily be perceived as coercion, as there is a negative connotation if the deadline is not met. Deadlines can concentrate the mind, but impose them with caution unless your intent is to raise the stakes. If a deadline is needed, be sure to explain the context, giving good reasons why it is necessary to curtail negotiations in this way.

Either way, threats are likely to provoke a negative and hostile reaction. Therefore, unless you want to raise the temperature of the talks, it is better to couch such statements as warnings of what may well result if the other side doesn't change its ways.

The first point is assessing where you are in the negotiations. Is the other side showing no indication of a willingness to move? Have you signalled your intention to move and implied the possibility of mutual concessions? Do they appear to have come to the negotiating table without a mandate for compromise? In other words, is there every reason to believe that your bottom lines do not overlap?

It can be counterproductive simply to carry on trying to bargain with an unresponsive opponent; better to apply pressure subtly and get real negotiations going. If this appears to be the situation, then there may well be a need to give a salutary reminder of the consequences of failing to reach agreement.

When you decide to apply pressure, the best advice is to do so gently and proportionately. As William Ury neatly puts it in *Getting Past No*:

"...use power to bring him to his senses, not his knees."

Machiavelli may not have agreed, but in employment relations negotiations, if not in war, restraint is prudent if you want to do business together in the future.

The aim should be to apply coercion gently at first. Then, don't immediately ratchet up the pressure, or you will simply increase their resistance. A better way is to apply pressure, then relax, before putting on the pressure again. Don't rush them, it is better if the other side come to the conclusion that they need to make a concession without further input from you.

However, having made an explicit threat, you can expect a negative response. The likely consequence is that the other side will reply with their own threat. Ignore it, keep calm (easier said than done!) and show that you are unfazed and remain positive. Note what they have said, restate your intention of getting a negotiated settlement and return to negotiations by restating your proposal and asking for their comments. If there is still no positive response again explore possible deadlock-breakers, before considering 'upping the ante' with a stronger threat.

However, before doing so, you need to be confident that you are not bluffing unintentionally. Negotiating teams can start believing their own propaganda so, before initiating coercive action, be certain that you can deliver and your perception of the power balance is correct. You might also want to check back with your constituents, to make sure that they will be behind you. Secondly, consider what they can do in response and how you can best counter it. Never threaten if you can't deliver. And, if you do decide to bluff, be prepared to have your bluff called.

What to do if you are threatened

As always, stay calm and professional. Do not respond emotionally but express your disappointment; in short, assume the moral high ground. What you must not do is be seen to respond by making a concession – if you do you will regret it. Instead, emphasise that you are here to talk and express the hope that, even at this late stage, the other side can be persuaded to pull back from these actions which will be damaging to everybody.

You will have anticipated this eventuality in your preparation and have arrangements prepared to minimise the impact of whatever coercion the other side may attempt. You should indicate this to the other side, saying that you will need to implement these in the interests of customers, the general public, etc. Then get back to the negotiations.

Like it or not, coercion is part of negotiation. Threats, overt or covert, reflect the pressure that negotiators are able to apply to their opponents because of the perceived power balance in the relationship. So expect threats and don't be fazed when you are threatened. Don't back down. If you do you will reward their use of threats and you will get more of the same in the future. Keep cool and, when faced with personal attacks, act even cooler.

Unless you want to escalate the situation, don't over-react, reply neutrally, indicating that you are well aware of this possibility. If you can respond to a threat by indicating that you are prepared for it, and its effects can be dealt with, then the other side's position will be weakened considerably. As long, of course, that this is not seen itself as a transparent bluff!

Bargaining from weakness

But, what should you do if you find yourself in a weak position? If the other side has the upper hand and is dictating the pace of the negotiations, you are at risk of being steamrollered into a bad agreement. It would be foolish to allow your side to be drawn into a deal that won't be acceptable to your constituents and on which you won't be able to deliver. You need to employ delaying tactics, but you don't want to be seen to be negative or be the cause of the negotiations breaking down.

You might find it useful at this point to compliment the other side on the force of their negotiating, saying that they have introduced some radical alternatives that are worthy of further consideration or that they have taken you beyond your current remit. Flattery is rarely wasted! Don't reveal that you have a weak hand. Make the discussions as informal as possible and get the other side to invest more in the relationship than they need to do the deal. It will be harder for them to use coercion if there appears to be a good relationship between you.

Now use adjournments, saying that you need time to consult your superiors (or in the case of trade unions, your executive committee) because you need, for example: to take legal advice, to speak to technical advisers, or to analyse the data. You may still be accused of dragging your feet and you do risk undermining your own authority as a decision maker. But, if you can get on friendly terms with the other side, they are less likely to say so overtly.

Having obtained a break in the negotiations, you should play it long. Use the time to regroup, then re-examine your options, develop alternative proposals and organise your next steps. Look again at the walk-away alternatives, both theirs and yours. It may be that they have more to lose by using coercion than it first appears. For example, employee representatives often underestimate the benefits to management of change being introduced by agreement rather than by imposition. If nothing else get them back into negotiations, consider making a minor concession, and keep talking. The moment for them to use coercion may have passed.

Breaking the deadlock

Negotiations often reach an impasse so be prepared. A deadlock can mark the turning point, after which the remaining areas of disagreement are soon resolved. But, failure to break the log jam is likely to be destructive to relationships; both sides will start digging in and any optimism that progress could be possible on other points will quickly evaporate.

But remember, deadlock may not be deadlock! It may be a bluff. If you suspect this, don't react, ignore it, carry on and wait for their reaction.

Alternatively, it may be that they are looking for something to get them off a hook. They may be mandated to hold to their current position, but privately recognise that it is unachievable. If you think this is the case, it may be worth offering a modest concession on something aside from the main issue, which they can then take back to their constituents and hopefully get a changed mandate.

William Ury, in *Getting Past No*, talks about "going around stone walls". The idea here is that you treat the other side's intractable position as their aspiration. They may be stuck on a hook, so recognise the position as what they want and invite them to talk about how you both can meet it.

Deadlocks in negotiations call for an indirect approach, as a direct assault will only result in the other side defending their position more strongly. Then the impasse will spread, with even previous areas of agreement at risk. This is where signalling comes in, because neither side will want to show weakness. So signal that mutual concessions might be possible by saying that you will look again at your position, if they agree to reflect on theirs. Of course, they may only offer something you would have expected to get anyway, but it is a start and you will have got the talks going again.

Other deadlock-breaking techniques include:

- Remind the other side of the likely consequences if the deadlock is not broken. However, this must not be done in an accusative manner. One way is to ask a leading question such as "what do you think will happen if we can't agree on this point?" The reply is likely to include a statement to the effect that "...and it will be your fault". Ignore that, simply underline the fact that neither you nor they want that outcome, and then return to the problem.
- Call for an adjournment. This will allow both sides time to reflect, consider their options and possibly draw back from their current position. Always use adjournments with a purpose and give the other side something to do with the

time, a proposition to consider or a range of possibilities to reflect on. With nothing else to do, the hawks in their camp may gain the upper hand and, when you meet again you may find that matters have worsened, not improved.

- Consider 'parking' the problem and moving on to next item. This may seem like ducking the issue (and it may be that it is too important to do this) but it is surprising how sometimes leaving an issues, only to return to it later, will free up entrenched positions. Often this is because, by then, you have built up a momentum towards settlement and previous disagreements no longer seem so intractable.

- Call a halt in proceeding for today, arrange to meet again tomorrow and, before then, make use of informal contacts so discover what needs to be done to get the talks back on track. For example, a telephone call with your opposite number or even a private, confidential meeting may do the trick. But arranging informal contacts may be difficult to arrange if trust levels are low. Another way of doing this is to make use of informal channels at a lower level in the organisation. It may be, for example, that a local manager is seen as trustworthy by a local rep. A conversation between these two might be a way of discovering what can be done.

- Offer to meet their lead negotiator for a private conversation. This tactic is commonly called a 'corridor meeting', although a side room is a better venue. The idea is that if these two are allowed to meet, one-on-one, plain speaking between the two, away from their respective team members, may be able to clear the way for more constructive talks. However, their team may not trust their lead negotiator sufficiently (or you may not trust yours!) because of fears that they will concede too much. This tactic needs to be used sparingly and at the right time. It is risky because it relies on the professionalism and integrity of the two respective lead negotiators. They must be able to trust each other to speak openly, be truthful and observe confidences. If one or both fall short of these standards, the damage done to the relationship may be irreparable.

- Try a new venue, different team members, bring in experts; anything that changes the current dynamics of the negotiations may break the deadlock.
- Escalate the situation by calling in the most senior representatives of each side. I call this "bringing in the grandparents". It is a tactic that can work because it shows to all concerned that everything is being done to resolve the dispute. There are however two potential downsides: firstly, the higher up the hierarchy you go, and no matter how able these senior players are, the more they will see the big picture and ignore the detail. Indeed, you will have trouble stopping them. But, with any negotiation, the devil is in the detail. As a result, "bringing in the grandparents" can break the deadlock and get a deal, but the price may be higher than they anticipated and you wanted. Secondly, their presence devalues your team's authority and sets a precedent for next time. Will you be able to reach a deal without them if the other side got more by holding out until, for example, the Chief Executive was called in?
- Brinkmanship has an important role in negotiation. If the deadlock is now so serious as to threaten the future of the talks and trigger a strike or a walkout, now is the time for a new idea. If you have been holding back that one concession or a different option, now is the time to introduce it. As in comedy, timing is everything. Having a trick up your sleeve by way of a valuable concession or a novel option, can break the deadlock and clinch the deal. It must be valuable to your opponent, (though not necessarily of high value to you). But be careful to play it at the right time and do so with apparent great reluctance. Once played, you will have nothing left and you can only play it once. So once you have decided to use it, aim to move to a resolution of the negotiations as quickly as possible.
- Call in a third-party (this is discussed further in the Chapter on Alternative Dispute Resolution).

Case Study 6

I was asked to assist in negotiating a trade union recognition agreement at an NHS Trust. From the start it was clear that the major hurdle to overcome was the principled stand being taken by one of the major trade unions.

I was told that it was Union policy not to sit at the same negotiating table as a smaller trade union which was not a member of the TUC. The union in question had satisfied the Certification Officer that is was an independent body and the employer now insisted that it must be recognised for collective bargaining purposes.

Needless to say, there was a history of rivalry between the two unions. I checked and found that, in fact, the two organisations did share a negotiating table in several other NHS Trusts around the country. The local representative went back and found that the position nationally was not quite as clear cut as he had been led to believe. A compromise proved possible and the two organisations were able to work together at local level.

Negotiating non-negotiable items

A particularly difficult type of deadlock can arise when you are told by the other side that no compromise can be made on an issue because it is "a matter of principle". Generally, however, in employee relations, even non-negotiable items can eventually be negotiated, provided the price is right and a climb down can be managed without too much loss of face.

Nevertheless, if it is a genuine principled stand and a concession really is not possible, then other tactics need to be explored. For example, the trade union rep may say that what you are saying is against national Union policy. If so, it pays to check, as the policy may be less clear and not as straightforward as it first appears.

One way of avoiding a damaging confrontation can be to use informal contacts to convince the other side of the seriousness of the situation. A private meeting of the lead negotiators, possibly with their bosses present (e.g. Managing Director and National Union Officer) can work around the issue.

Through such an off-the-record conversation you might even find that, although agreement to the change is not possible, the Union might, under protest, reluctantly accept imposition without going into dispute.

Another way forward might be the involvement of an independent third party like Acas. Provided all parties agree, Acas will get involved even if the formal machinery has yet to be exhausted. Conciliation will seek to resolve the impasse and get a return to normal negotiations.

Whatever else happens, keep calm; maintain an exterior of optimism and positivity. When the going gets tough others will feed off your energy. Without it negativity will spread throughout your team and theirs. And, yes, it can get worse!

Ultimately, however, if both sides need to reach agreement, even the most stubborn deadlock will be resolved. If the situation is serious enough, and only in the last resort, it may be that coercion will be needed. It may be that imposition is the only way forward. Indeed there have been occasions when a trade union has informally told an employer to impose a deal as they could not be seen to agree it. The members then will be required to 'put up or shut up'. But such matters are best dealt with privately, away from the formality of the negotiating table and require the lead negotiators to trust in the confidentiality of a private conversation.

As we have seen, a negotiator must understand the reality of the power relationship in their workplace and be prepared to use the threat of coercion, and respond proportionately to threats from the other side. They must be prepared to encounter and overcome apparent intractable deadlocks and maintain the momentum of the negotiations. Having done this, the next step will be to reach a deal.

6

END GAME

"If there's not any endgame, we're in quicksand. We take one more step, and we're still there, and there's no way out."
Richard Shelby

We are now close to concluding a deal. This chapter will explore how this can be done without making unnecessary concessions or without talks breaking down at the last minute. Most importantly it will look at how we can ensure that the deal reached will stand the test of time.

Closing the deal

"I'm a compromiser and a manoeuvrer. I try to get 'something'. That's the way our system works."
Lyndon B Johnson

As you start to move into closing the deal, don't give the game away by showing yourself be too eager. Indeed, you should appear reluctant. Every indication you give out should convey the message that you have moved as much as you can and that you have little or nothing left to give.

In particular be cautious about going into too much detail, too quickly. If you, or a team member, are drawn into discussions about the finer points of a deal before the principles have been agreed, you are in effect saying that the deal is done. But it may not be and you may find that you find yourself making further concessions unnecessarily. You must be particularly sensitive to what they are saying before deciding that now is the time to clinch the deal.

Timing is everything but there will come a point when it is time to stop negotiating. At this stage, don't make the mistake of trying to drive too hard a bargain. If you do, you will breed resentment and they will resist proper implementation of the deal. They will want revenge and, the next time you have to negotiate, they will do their best to get it.

When you decide to make your final offer, keep it businesslike; give it in short sentences, with not many supporting arguments. Make it clear that there are no more concessions to be had. Use words like "this is all I've got." Of course, in employment relations negotiating, there are often more than one such offer and final, final offers are not uncommon. But, to maintain your integrity, avoid repeating the 'F' word. Once you get a reputation for moving from your final position, you will be expected to do so ever after. 'Never say never', but avoid it if you possibly can, and if you do move, always move with good reason for specific objectives.

This may be a good time to put what you consider will be the deal in writing. There are pluses and minuses here: if it is complicated, with detailed figure work, then it may be worth it to ensure the other side understands exactly what is in the final offer. Indeed, it may save time later, as this draft can be used to produce the final agreement. However, the down side is that drafting and exchanging documents is time consuming. Producing and examining drafts will slow down the pace and impetus of a negotiation.

When you reach the point where you have been given an offer that you think your side can live with and is the best you can get, don't react, never ever appear eager. Even if they accept your offer, be cautious. Take a deep breath, pause and reflect: you won't have got all you wanted but, ask yourself, "Have I got enough of what I need?"

By all means, take your time and gather your thoughts, but don't let the moment slip. Don't keep the other side waiting too long as, whilst you are delaying, the hawks in their camp may be gaining the upper hand. If they do, when you go back in, the deal will no longer be on the table and some, possibly spurious, reason will be offered as to why this is the case. Equally, if you react too quickly, the other side will feel they have moved too much and seek to retract from their position. Either way, it is one step forward, two steps back.

When I knew that one side had passed an offer to me that the other side would almost certainly accept, I walked down the corridor between the two rooms very slowly. I used to say "I think I can get them to offer this..." After I had been told that this would do the deal, I walked back down the corridor even more slowly. I knew that, if the deal was to stick, both sides had to know that they had gone the extra mile and that they couldn't have achieved any more.

Knowing when to stop negotiating can be a difficult decision but it is one that must be made and getting it wrong will have serious consequences. To go on too long can be self-defeating: I have seen many negotiations founder because the negotiators didn't know how to say 'yes'. Equally, negotiators must have stamina and persistence and not lose a war of attrition.

In making this decision, you will need to assess the benefits of acceptance against the likely consequences of agreement not being reached. How does it compare to your negotiating plan? How does it compare to your walk away alternative? A good trick is to call an adjournment and, in the privacy of your team room, convert the latest position into hard cash. By this point in the process you may have been talking percentages or headline figures for so long that you may have lost sight of the overall picture; the difference between you may now be quite small, certainly compared to the cost of not reaching a deal.

Before going back to the negotiating table, check with your team members that they will sign up to the deal and support you in selling it to those you represent. It is a regrettable fact that some of your own team members may try to distance themselves from the less attractive aspects of a deal. You need to enforce team discipline at this point and subsequently. If you have strayed beyond your mandate, check back before speaking again to the other side (to do otherwise will diminish your authority in their eyes).

When you get back to the negotiating table, it is vital to make sure that it is not a false dawn: use summarising and directive questioning to check that you understand (and they understand) exactly what is being proposed. It may well be that there is still some way to go.

One thing you can be assured of, once details of the deal you have concluded gets out, you will be accused of having moved too far or of selling out. Accept it, it comes with the territory! Compromise is not necessarily a bad thing if everyone can live with it and all concerned can back down and save face. I have concluded a few deals that I knew were little more than 'shoddy compromises' but they were necessary at the time to allow the parties to move on. If you do compromise, make sure you know you are doing it and understand the likely implications.

Let's split the difference

One option you may have is to split the difference, and provided the difference between you is now small compared to the cost of not reaching agreement, then it may be a price you can pay. But, this tactic must only be used as part of the end game, and then only used once, so don't propose or agree to this unless you are sure it will finalise the deal. Make absolutely sure that they will come half way to meet you before you commit to "split the difference", otherwise you risk making an offer that cannot then be unsaid.

If you do it, emphasise the size of the concessions you have already made. A problem here is that the parties will never agree who has conceded the most. So when it comes to splitting the difference, one side will always feel that they are being asked to go even farther than the other side to get agreement. If this is the case, splitting the difference will not feel equitable and, even if it clinches the deal, there may still be problems ahead. As ever, go back to you negotiating plan, cost what is proposed (both to you and to them) before making a decision.

Put it in writing

The closure of lengthy negotiations brings with it the risk of mistakes being made. By this stage the parties can be feeling a mix of emotions: elation, exhaustion, and frustration. Above all they will want to finish the proceedings and go home. It is not surprising therefore that there can be an unwillingness to subject the putative agreement to detailed scrutiny, yet this is what is needed at this final stage.

Time must now be spent drafting, editing and agreeing a document that sets out precisely what has been agreed, together with how and when it will be implemented. Team members may be reluctant to go this extra mile, so it will be the job of the lead negotiators to keep them on task, as it is vital that all concerned have ownership of the final agreement.

Case Study 7

A colleague of mine in Acas once made a classic mistake. She had been conciliating in a local dispute and the talks went on until late in the evening. Eventually, however, agreement was reached and, because of the late hour, the parties agreed to meet again the following day to draw up the agreement.

Inevitably, overnight both sides reflected on the deal they had reached. The Managing Director decided that he had been too generous. Similarly, the Union negotiator reflected that he should have held out for more. When they met again, the agreement they had reached the night before had vanished. Both parties wanted to reopen negotiations and both tried to blame the conciliator! Far from a swift resolution, the dispute became even more intractable and recriminatory. I learned from her mistake and have always insisted on holding the parties together until the deal is formally signed up.

As ever, 'the devil is in the detail' and this is the last opportunity to resolve any potential misunderstandings which could otherwise emerge, to disastrous effect, in the subsequent communication and implementation phases. In particular make sure that the terms used are defined, for example: 'What does pay constitute?' 'What is the operative date?' 'How exactly will the phasing operate?' Don't forget, even if all of those present know what is meant, for implementation to be successful, everyone affected must understand the agreement, so check the drafting for jargon or obscure language.

Case Study 8

I was involved in a dispute over the meaning of a collective agreement. The local shop steward took it to mean that all changes on the shop floor must be subject to negotiation and therefore would not, for example, accept the introduction of new product lines unless these were agreed in advance with the Union. The local manager said that the company would never have signed up to this. He would always be happy discuss minor changes; he insisted that he would only negotiate on substantive issues like pay, bonuses and hours of work.

When I met the Chief Executive and the Union Full-time Officer, I found they both agreed with local management. Yet, a literal reading of the agreement supported the steward's interpretation. The wording of the agreement did not accurately reflect the intentions of its signatories.

It was very difficult for the Union to back down, as relationships at the site had now deteriorated badly, and the steward was looking for the support of her Full-time Officer. Matters were resolved, but not without some damaged relationships at local level.

The feel of the meeting should now be one of co-operation and problem-solving and the adversarial phase should now be almost completed. However, it is possible at this point that negotiators, on both sides of the table, start to have cold feet over the proposed deal, or even that they should have asked for more and conceded less.

If this is the case, an adjournment should be called and the lead negotiators need to re-establish consensus and ensure team discipline.

Also at this late stage negotiators may try to secure more through 'brinkmanship'. This can border on 'dirty tricks' and will be discussed in more detail later. Again, the lead negotiator needs to remain calm and insist that what has been agreed remains agreed.

Nevertheless, should joint scrutiny discovers that genuine, fundamental differences of interpretation remain unresolved, the parties will have no alternative but to go back a stage and, after an adjournment, return to the bargaining process. Negotiators should here be alert to the temptation to fudge a remaining obstacle as the final price of a resolution. The implementation of deals done in this manner can be doomed to failure when the wording comes under the scrutiny of those outside of the negotiating room.

One consolation is that, whilst resources will always be at a premium, the supply of words is unlimited. The temptation to fudge must be resisted but the use of language in the presentation of a deal can provide a means to allow the deal to be more readily acceptable. It is worth listening to what the other side says because the words used can make the difference between acceptance and rejection. Rejection of a deal reached at the bargaining table by a ballot of the workforce is the worst of all worlds. How the deal is described and presented can avoid this, so time is well worth investing in discussing the wording.

The outcome of the scrutiny process should be an agreed document that will now form the basis of all future communications. Communicating the deal to the workforce should be the joint responsibility of managers and employee representatives. It is also particularly important that communications with line managers are a feature of this process. Employer side negotiators need to appreciate that the trade union will now need to sell the deal to its members. It can be well worth employers assisting them in this process by providing them with the necessary facilities if this will help the membership ballot returning a positive outcome. Facilities can take the form of time off to address meetings of the membership, venues for such meetings, access to electronic media, etc. In some situations joint presentations by union and management negotiators, using pre-prepared scripts and Q&A briefs, can smooth the path to acceptance and implementation.

The theatre of signing

As a conciliator, whenever I had concluded a deal I always got the parties to sign it off. In reality, this ceremony had little meaning. In almost all cases the 'agreement' would now be the subject of a membership ballot and the best I could hope for was that part of the agreement would be that the union negotiators would recommend it for acceptance. Nevertheless, I felt that the 'theatre of signing' was always worthwhile because it underlined that, usually after much effort by all concerned, the parties had succeeded in getting a deal, the parties had ownership of it and were committed to its implementation.

This must not be the time for triumph or celebration on your part. Even if the other side announce the deal as a great victory, you must not react. Remember, presentation is everything and this may be a price you have to pay to get the deal you wanted. It can be possible, at this stage, to have a frank discussion with the other side about your respective needs when it comes to publicising the deal. The reality of the situation may be that the other side need to avoid losing face and, even if it is their fault for raising their constituents' expectations too high, they may need your forbearance if the deal is to be accepted.

In the words of Sun Tzu, the 6th century BC Chinese General and military strategist:

> *"To a surrounded enemy, you must leave a way of escape. Build your opponent a golden bridge to retreat across."*

It is not easy to be self-effacing, especially after long and, at times, heated negotiations. What is more, if the other side are triumphal, you will have to explain this to your constituents (who may be feeling more than a little bruised by the experience). You will then need to issue a measured and non-controversial public response. In any adversarial situations, the competitive spirit can run high and, not surprisingly, you want to come out on top. As a negotiator once said to me, "I'm all in favour of a win-win solution, provided of course that we win more!" Regrettably, even if privately you know that you have indeed 'won more', it will be imprudent and counterproductive to say so publicly.

Implementing the deal

It is not unusual for there to be problems with the implementation of a deal. Those around the bargaining table may have lived and breathed it, but those outside of the negotiations will not necessarily have buy-in; crucially, however, it is these individuals who will be needed to make the deal work. If time has been spent on the wording of the agreement and in communicating it to all concerned, then you are less likely to have difficulties. A further precaution is to agree, as part of the deal, an implementation plan, setting out who will do what and by when. It can be difficult keeping the parties together for this final task, but it is worth it if it saves time and trouble later.

Despite all your endeavours, it can still all go wrong even at this late stage, especially if certain key players on one or both sides are working against it. If this happens, the lead negotiators from both sides need to meet again urgently for some frank discussions. Remember, not only is the deal at stake, with all that may imply, but their relationship and authority in future negotiations is now at risk.

Review

In any significant business project it would be standard practice to hold a review after implementation. Yet, in my experience, it is rare for this to be done with a negotiation. Nevertheless, there is much that could be learned from an evaluation. For example, how did the planning hold up? Did it prove sufficient or were there events that should have been anticipated? Were the objectives set at the outset achieved? Did the tactics you planned to use work? How did the team perform? What were its successes and the failures? And, perhaps the most important of all, what will you do differently next time?

Of course, if you have gone further down the road of Win-Win bargaining, you might like to hold a joint review, involving both parties to the negotiation. If there is sufficient trust and openness, I am sure that this would be very revealing, but I've never seen it done.

To help you review your own personal performance as a negotiator, in the appendix to this book is a simple self-analysis tool to see how you shape up. It should sum up the good practice we have been discussing in the last few chapters.

The next chapter, however, is not about good practice; it is about dirty tricks. But, trickery has its place in a negotiator's armoury, even if only to prepare you for what the other side might try next.

7

DIRTY TRICKS

"... our experience has been that those princes who have done great things have held good faith of little account, and have known how to circumvent the intellect of men by craft, and in the end have overcome those who have relied on their word."
Niccolo Machiavelli

"It's better to get something worthwhile done using deception than to fail to get something worthwhile done using truth."
Don Juan

This chapter gives some examples of 'dirty tricks' in negotiating — how to play them, how to spot them, how to respond and the risks involved.

As we have seen, in employment relations, traditional negotiations are inherently conflictual. Both sides want to do well for their constituents; indeed, they may be under considerable pressure to be seen to do so. It is no surprise therefore that some negotiators, on occasions, seek to gain advantage by deception or trickery. It could even be argued that, since persuasion is about disguising the full facts of your case, and exaggerating the benefits, then all negotiation is based on trickery.

What you choose to do so is up to you. But, if your opponent recognises a trick, and regards it as unethical, any reputation you had for integrity will have been lost. It can take years to build up trust, but only five minutes to knock it down. It depends whether you value the relationship or, more pragmatically, whether you will need to do business together again.

So what do you do if you spot a 'Dirty Trick' being played on you? If you expose your opponent openly as a trickster, although they have been caught out, the response is likely to be defensive and aggressive. Whatever personal pleasure you may get will be outweighed by the damage done to the relationship.

Nevertheless, you need to show your opponent that, by trying to trick you, he is making a mistake and, as Napoleon Bonaparte said:

"Never interrupt your enemy when he is making a mistake."

A better response, therefore, is more subtle: relax, wait, question gently and seek to signal that you know what they tried to do, but you aren't deceived. This way you have allowed the other side not to lose face, but your reputation as a negotiator has been enhanced. You have gained the advantage.

Loaded questions

However you answer a loaded question can weaken your position. For example: "So what you are saying is that you want us to finance the pay increase with job cuts?"

So, unless you can do so authoritatively and concisely, answer with a question – question the question. So, unless you can say: "We are not cutting jobs", respond by asking: "So what savings can be made to finance the pay increase?"

Inaccurate summarising

Listen very carefully when the other side summarises. They may deliberately add in points that have been discussed but certainly not agreed. If you miss this and try and rectify the situation later, you will be accused of backtracking. And watch that you are accurate in your summarising, or you will be accused of dirty tricks.

Linked to this tactic is the equally duplicitous trick of pretending to have misunderstood – the error, of course, will always be in their favour. When corrected, they will claim to have made an honest mistake, perhaps even suggesting that you were in some way responsible. Deliberate misunderstanding can be an 'irritator', designed to throw you off your stride; as a delaying tactic; or, as an attempt to revisit agreed items and win further concessions.

Whatever their motivation may be, react calmly and be prepared to take a step backwards and correct any 'misunderstandings'. But don't accuse the other side of foul play unless you deliberately want to turn up the heat or provoke a breakdown.

Silence

It is rarely a good idea to react quickly either to a question or to a proposal made by the other side, as a pause will indicate thoughtfulness and show that you are giving proper consideration to a suggestion. What is more, it gives you a moment to think! But a silence of only a few seconds can also be a powerful way of putting pressure on the other side. It can make them uncomfortable, perhaps make them think that they have said something foolish and they may fall into the trap of filling in the gap by giving something away. However, like many such tactics, this can easily be overdone. They can be seen for what they are and show up the other side as merely games players.

So, if silence is used on you, recognise it as being a dirty trick, but don't rise to the bait. If you find it excessive and unsettling, a strong response would be to say something like: "I can see that you are hesitant. Perhaps you weren't prepared for this line of approach. Would you like an adjournment to allow you to gather your thoughts?" Having confronted this behaviour, it is unlikely that they will try it on you twice.

Bite their hand off

This trick is intended to throw the other side off balance by saying yes to their opening offer. The offer may be ridiculously low, but it is 'accepted' because so many strings are added to the 'acceptance' as to make it unacceptable to the other side. Included amongst these caveats are some that you would be happy to give away. This tactic can be high risk and needs thorough preparation and a detailed counter offer. But it can free-up previously rigid positional thinking.

For example management might say they would accept the high pay settlement sought by the union, but their "price" would be acceptance of radical changes to working practices. In practice these are rarely acceptable in their entirety, but it may allow compromise on a level of trade-off that would otherwise unlikely to have been considered.

Creating deadlock

Creating deadlock can be a deliberate move. For example, when the other side's expectations are so high, desperate measures may be needed to confront these and manage them downwards. One way of doing this is to manoeuvre to create a deadlock, possibly even getting the other side to walk out.

This can be done by getting your retaliation in first: present your opening position in uncompromising terms, giving no hint of room for movement. Construct your opening position so that it is well in excess of what you expect to settle at. Express, in strong terms, your horror and disbelief at their opening position.

The idea is that, when they show signs of moving, you can respond positively (albeit appearing very reluctant to do so) because you have built in plenty of headroom. You can then claim that you have moved significantly and expect them now to match it with further concessions of their own.

Needless to say, it is a high risk policy which could end in deadlock and conflict, so be prepared to live with the consequences. Secondly, your extreme opening position must still be capable of appearing credible; if it is not, your tactic will be seen to be the bluff that it is. This is not a trick to try too often!

Just one more thing...

Columbo, the 1970s TV Detective played by Peter Falk, had a clever technique when interviewing suspects. Just as he was leaving, he would turn and say "just one more thing..." This invariably seemed to catch the guilty person out.

Negotiators use a variation of this trick – I call it the 'Columbo tactic' and it is one of my favourites but it requires good timing. Just when you think that everything is resolved, the other side will say "just one more thing..." and come up with what they would have you believe is only a minor matter, but they will make the deal contingent upon you conceding the point. I have known this played so successfully, that it transpired that there was more than one "just one more thing". If challenged, the negotiator will look hurt and suggest that you surely cannot object to such a minor point when there is so much at stake!

A variation on this theme is where particularly manipulative negotiators try to get you to agree to a list of demands, one after the other, whilst avoiding making any firm commitment themselves, or even reopening what you had thought had been settled.

Faced with this tactic, you need to regain control of the negotiation by insisting that an exhaustive list of issues is drawn up first and then worked through. You can then play them at their own game, by listening to and discussing all their demands, but refusing to agree anything until everything is on the table.

Agenda overload

Similar to Columbo, the Agenda Overload tactic can be a ploy to get more out of a negotiation by wearing the other side down. In this situation, however, right from the outset one side adds a long list of items to the negotiation agenda, most of which are minor matters. Essentially time wasting, this tactic can work well when there are external deadlines imposed on the negotiations.

Although frustrating, countering this ploy needs patience and determination. You need to demonstrate that you too can be there for the long haul. It will require persistence, but you need to identify which items really matter to the other side and which are merely 'fillers'. Then explain that, as everything has a cost, any offer on these minor points will result in a reduced offer on the main points. Suggest that, if they agree to remove these items, you might be able to do something on the substantive issues (which of course you would have done anyway). Another tactic that may be worth trying is to attempt to divert some of these extraneous items to other forums (for example, working groups, existing consultative bodies, or separate talks).

It will also help your position considerably if the deadlines imposed on the negotiations can be removed or significantly extended. You might for example suggest that, if negotiations are delayed this could mean that the eventual settlement level may be lower as backdating cannot be guaranteed. This of course is a threat and quite possibly a bluff, so a degree of caution may be needed.

Are you having a laugh?

As already noted, humour, providing it is appropriate and not over done, can be a good way of dispelling tension and building rapport. Used another way, however, it can be an offensive weapon and a deliberate dirty trick.

Incredulous laughter can be used as a response with the deliberate intent of ridiculing the offer and undermining the other side's position. Combined with mannerisms like throwing the pen down, raising eyebrows and turning to team in apparent disbelief, it can be a tactic that is unnerving and difficult to deal with. Its one drawback, however, is that it is so over-used that it quickly loses its impact.

Faced with such intentionally infantile behaviour, you have a choice of responses depending on how you assess your bargaining position. If you fear an early breakdown of talks, a neutral reaction is perhaps the safest; so ignoring the provocation and continuing with your game plan would be the best way forward. A stronger response would be to say something like: "from your reaction, you don't appear to appreciate the seriousness of the situation, so perhaps you would like an adjournment to regain your composure and consider your position?" If, however, you are comfortable with the possibility of a breakdown, an even stronger response would be to indicate that you will walk out if they are not prepared to take matters seriously. This however would be a high risk strategy.

Good cop, bad cop

Despite perhaps the oldest dirty trick in the world, and therefore the easiest to spot, it is remarkable how well this tactic can work. Two negotiators work in tandem, taking turns to lead, with one taking an over-aggressive, hard line, whilst the other appearing by comparison to be more reasonable and collaborative. Its purpose, of course, is to unsettle negotiators. Because we are concerned that the 'bad cop' will have the final say in the negotiation, we fall into the trap of believing that the apparently friendly 'good cop' is doing his best for us. The temptation is to do the deal on the 'good cop's' terms, because that is all we can get. After all, he is really on our side isn't he?

An experienced negotiator will refuse to play this game. The sensible response is to try and play one off against the other; reflect back 'amusement' at such overt games playing; and, even suggest that other side might like an adjournment to get their act together, as it would appear that they aren't speaking with one voice. You might even make a joke of it, saying something like: "this feels a bit like good cop, bad cop. I hope you two aren't going to get typecast!"

Of course it is possible that this isn't a trick, but actually a reflection of the genuine personalities of the two individuals concerned! Either way, it is easily dealt with.

And, whether accompanied by Mr Nasty or not, don't be fooled by Mr Nice Guy. Many negotiators are genuinely nice, likeable people and they can make very effective negotiators. When faced with a nice guy, the temptation is to relax your guard: it is always more difficult to disagree with a nice guy.

Finally, don't make the assumption that all bad behaviour is a deliberate dirty trick. You may be exaggerating the abilities of your opponent. What appears to be a tactic may be little more than inexperience or incompetence. Either way, respond appropriately and seek to use their behaviour to your advantage.

8

HANDLING AGGRESSION

"The tendency of aggression is an innate, independent, instinctual disposition in man... it constitutes the most powerful obstacle to culture."
Sigmund Freud

Negotiations can get personal and be very stressful. You can face personal attacks, emotional outbursts and aggressive behaviour. This chapter looks at how you should respond and even turn the situation to your advantage.

Personal attacks

Aggressive behaviour and personal insults are hard to take. You will feel them to be an attack on your self-esteem, disrespectful to you as a negotiator, to your position in the organisation and to you as an individual. Why should you have to take this sort of behaviour? You don't and it isn't acceptable; but, how you deal with it will say a lot about you as a negotiator.

Fisher & Ury, in their excellent *Getting to Yes*, say that personal attacks should be treated as attacks on the problem; good advice but not always easy to follow. You will feel stressed. We all know the symptoms: your stomach knots up, you might blush, your hand may even shake slightly and a slight stammer can come into your voice in your voice. Less obvious is that our heart rate increases and the adrenaline levels in our body are raised. All this is perfectly natural, as is your desire to respond in kind. But, if you allow yourself to get angry, you risk losing self-control.

As Ambrose Bierce, the American writer and satirist put it:

"Speak when you are angry, and you will make the best speech you will ever regret."

Rather, turn the situation to your benefit, get your opponent off-balance and perhaps they will let slip something to your advantage.

The best way forward therefore is to pause, perhaps write a note (as if recording the insult), become very cool, make eye contact and repeat the question or respond with a statement about the issue (but don't refer directly to the personal attack). The aim is to make the other side worry that they have gone too far this time. Implicitly, you are showing them that they have behaved unprofessionally but don't say so openly, that risks further escalation and a spiral of attacks and counter-attacks.

If you find that you, or a member of your team, are losing self-control, then call for a short adjournment, and leave the room. On return, say something like "where were we, ah yes, you were explaining your concerns. Do you wish to say any more on this at this stage?"

Your aim at this point is to let them exhaust themselves whilst keeping in control yourself. All being well, they will blow themselves out, as it is hard to maintain aggression for extended periods. If it is simply their negotiator playing to the gallery then, having said their pre-planned piece, they will be able to get on with the business in hand. If the aggression is symptomatic of their mental state, their hostility reflects an underlying uncertainty and fear. You can use this to your advantage when, by careful, non-accusatory questioning, you probe their interests and concerns.

But first, you need to defuse the situation by your calmness and professionalism. Your body language and tone of voice must be saying that you will not be fazed by this behaviour, as you have seen it all before, but you are here to do business.

Then, let them talk; they clearly need to get all this off their chest, so you can even encourage them to unload. Catharsis means an emotional purging of deep seated and repressed emotions bringing relief. Hopefully, once their outburst has run its course, they will feel better for it and be more able to behave rationally. Catharsis also means an opening of the bowels by a strong laxative: the result is much the same.

Treat such displays as a sign of weakness and exploit it by seizing the moral high ground, saying things like "I can see you are upset, would you like a break?" When the outburst comes from a junior member of the other side's team, ask their lead negotiator "does your side need an adjournment?" The implicit criticism is far more powerful that a public challenge to the behaviour. Indeed, to confront crudely such outbursts will only rally the other side behind their leader.

If they get emotional, one tactic is to calmly acknowledge their strong feelings. In fact, until you do this, they will be reluctant to move on to discussing a solution. So say things like "I can see that you are genuinely angered by this" or "I do understand why this is of concern to you" or "I understand how you feel, I'd probably feel the same way myself. Let's find a way of doing something about it we can both live with." You are not agreeing with them or conceding ground, but you are showing that you are listening.

It is possible to go further and, without admission of blame, say something like "if that is the case, that wasn't our intention" or even "I'm sorry if we have caused you this concern, perhaps we can address this in these negotiations". Having reduced the emotional intensity of the discussions, and set a good example by your behaviour, you will be well placed to take the negotiations forward.

If you feel you must respond, say how you are feeling, not what they are doing. For example, "I feel I am being threatened" not "You are threatening me". Whatever you do, do not get drawn to a battle about what has happened in the past; rather, focus on the future and talk about how "we" can put things right.

You may feel that, by following this advice, you are implicitly condoning bad behaviour, and this may be true. However, your main aim is to conclude a deal that is beneficial to you. You want to be able to reward good behaviour and penalise bad behaviour in the course of a negotiation, but this is very difficult to achieve. A better course of action would be to address this issue once the negotiations have been concluded. For example you could offer a joint review of the negotiations once emotions have cooled. You may need to bring in other parties to achieve this, for example, an independent facilitator or trainer. Acas provides just such services.

Finally, there can be occasions when bad behaviour has a legitimate purpose. All negotiators need, on occasions, to play to the gallery and show their constituents how committed they are to the cause. Team members represent constituents and factions who expect the other side to be given a rough time. Lead negotiators may do the shooting, but their supporters provide the bullets and they expect to see them being fired. Sometimes the language used and positions expressed may be unhelpful to building rapport with the other side and risk provoking an equally hostile response. Nevertheless, such words may need to be seen to be said. There are times when whole such exchanges are staged managed with both sides feeling they need to put on a display for their constituents. This may seem like a ritual, but some rituals need to be observed. If you suspect this, you might consider why, at this particular time, the negotiator feels the need to use this tactic.

You also need to consider whether the outburst is a deliberate tactic aimed at provoking a breakdown of negotiations or justifying a walk out.

Either way, do not overreact, stay calm, and show that you, at least, are a professional. This is not simply point scoring, it actually builds up your negotiating power by weakening the other side's confidence and self-image.

Dealing with stress

"Stress: The confusion created when one's mind overrides the body's basic desire to choke the living daylights out of some jerk who desperately deserves it."
Unknown

As we have seen, negotiating is inherently stressful. Negotiators are under pressure to succeed, not just for themselves but for their 'side'. The outcome of the negotiations can be very serious for the organisation, for those they represent and, potentially for them as individuals.

Case Study 9

I conciliated in a dispute in a food processing company. The HR Director had been instructed to achieve flexible working practices as the price for the annual pay increase that year. The Union negotiators' mandate was not to accept any strings on the deal and balloted for industrial action. After lengthy talks, the resulting deal was a compromise: management agreed not to pursue flexible working that year; the Union agreed to only a low basic pay increase, and a bitter dispute was averted.

The HR Director took me to one side and said how relieved he was to secure a deal, as he knew his job would have been at risk if agreement had not been reached. I later learned that he had been dismissed a few weeks later; the deal hadn't been good enough for the Board.

Individuals can therefore have a lot at stake: they worry their careers are at risk; their self-image feels under attack, and they fear letting their side down. Negotiators on both sides of the table become emotionally committed to achieving a positive outcome. The pressures on negotiators can be excessive and can trigger both physical and emotional responses. It is not surprising then if negotiators occasionally act irrationally. Even senior negotiators can display some very dysfunctional behaviour; I've seen tears, threats, infantile behaviour and lots of bad language – it isn't common, but it happens.

Case Study 10

I nicknamed one Full-time Union Officer I dealt with regularly the "Ticking Bomb". He was an experienced negotiator, but he had one bad habit, in every difficult negotiation he would

---

> explode with anger. I knew he would do it, so I watched for
> the signs and tried to get the parties in separate rooms before
> it happened. One intemperate outburst could destroy all the
> progress that had been made over many hours.
>
> But on one occasion he flew into a rage after he had signed
> the agreement! At first I thought that it was just a negotiating
> tactic, but if it was, it was one that was counterproductive. I
> concluded that it was just his way of coping with the pressure.

Negotiating is therefore an emotional business and this dimension
needs to be understood and dealt with. Sometimes referred to
as 'emotional intelligence', a good negotiator can recognise and
understand emotions in other people, manage them in themselves,
and harness the emotional content of a situation to influence its
outcome.

By being aware of the other side's emotional triggers, a good
negotiator can use them to present their case to best effect. Some
individuals are no doubt born with greater emotional intelligence
than others. But most writers on the subject seem to suggest that
it can be learned and enhanced with training and practice. For a
negotiator, the place to start must be self-awareness and control of
their emotional responses.

As already noted, it can be difficult to resist reacting to outbursts
of anger but, unless you want to provoke a breakdown in the
negotiations, you must be able to take these in your stride.

You should also watch for signs of stress, both in yourself and in
your team, and have strategies ready to deal with this to prevent it
affecting the performance of your team. What you cannot tolerate
is one of your team going off script, either in their language or
their behaviour. Your first thought should be to call for a prompt
adjournment to allow you to regroup and them to regain composure.
A break will usually lower the tension; walk around the block, then
come back and start again. If this is not sufficient, consider a change
of team roles or even a change of team members. Team discipline
must be maintained if you are not to lose credibility.

Be aware, however that, if the other side have identified that you are having a problem with one of your team they will try and exploit it by targeting the individual. Neither you nor the team member must react. The other risk is that, if you are working to a tight deadline, the other side may assume that you are deliberately time wasting.

One of the biggest barriers to getting a deal is that one or both sides fear losing face. The longer a dispute goes on, the more likely it is that those involved have adopted fixed positions in which they have invested considerable time, energy and emotional commitment in building up. To retreat now would involve them in loss of face, status and prestige in the eyes of the other side, their own side, and their bosses. In such high pressure situations, it is therefore essential to give the other side a way out and help them sell the deal to their constituents. Indeed, independent third parties like Acas are often able resolve disputes because their involvement changes the dynamic and allow the negotiators to back down gracefully: 'getting negotiators off of hooks' would be a good job description for a conciliator.

Handling walkouts

Finally, one form of aggression that is not uncommon in workplace negotiations is the walk out. One side decides that the talks are going nowhere and stages a walk out. Often this is a sign that the 'hawks' in their camp have gained the upper hand. It can feel very satisfying to make this dramatic gesture and it can play well with your constituents. However, whilst it is easy to walk out, unless the other side publicly capitulates (which is unlikely) it can be very difficult to walk back in again. The problem is the potential for loss of face if you subsequently return to the negotiating table without first securing a tangible concession. Of course, the other side will be very resistant to giving any such thing for fear of giving in to pressure and being seen to be weak themselves. So walking-out runs a real risk of hardening an already difficult the situation. It is not therefore a tactic to be recommended, attractive though it might seem on occasions.

Should however the other side walk-out of the negotiations, it can be very hard not to respond angrily but, needless to say, you must not. As ever, keep calm, do not raise the temperature further, but seek to use the situation to your advantage. Use the media (internal and external) to express your regret; emphasise that you remain willing to talk at any time; and, by implication only, cast them as the guilty party. Of course, it may be your obstinacy in the negotiations that has prompted the breakdown, and you may need to reflect on this, but in all you say and do portray yourself as reasonable and moderate.

You now need to make it easy for them to come back to the negotiating table. The first step is to open informal contacts with the other side and suggest to them that confidential 'talks about talks' might be a way forward. Involving Acas or some other third-party might be another. What you are seeking to do here is to indicate to them, without commitment, where you think movement might be possible if the negotiations were resumed. Then explore how you can help them return to the negotiations without them being seen to be backing down. This may require some subtlety, and it may feel like rewarding bad behaviour, but the point is to get a deal not to humiliate them. Do not make any concessions, but a joint statement indicating both parties willingness to try again, in the interests of the company, the workforce and the customers, might do the trick.

Dealing with aggression is not easy but it is part of negotiating so expect it and deal with it. The next chapter looks at what is perhaps the most stressful challenge a negotiator can face: negotiating during industrial action.

9

NEGOTIATING YOUR WAY THROUGH A MAJOR DISPUTE

The purpose of this chapter is to look at some of the problems that can arise when you are negotiating your way through a major dispute. A section is included on managing the media. The chapter ends by looking at what can be done at the end of a major dispute to prevent similar problems in the future.

What to watch for

Major disputes can be very destructive, both to the organisation and to relationships in the workplace; the ill feeling they generate can last for years after the dispute has been resolved. Words said in the heat of a dispute cannot be unsaid, and trust and mutual respect may never be recovered. So, both managers and employee representatives need to be mentally prepared for such disputes and seek to act professionally despite all the pressures that are heaped upon them.

The longer a dispute runs, the greater will be the pressure on you from your constituents. Whether it is the Board, the parent company, customers, other employees, the media, or even politicians, everyone will want to know what you are doing, and why you haven't resolved it.

With no apparent resolution in sight both sides will be increasingly hard to resist the spiral of sanctions and counter-sanctions. Management will be under pressure to abandon negotiation and take ever more punitive measures: impose contractual changes, take legal action (injunctions for example), make dismissals, shutdown businesses, etc.

Such situations are rare and strikes even rarer; nevertheless, industrial action does get called and, be it an indefinite stoppage or, more likely, a series of shorter stoppages or an overtime ban, they pose particular problems for negotiators. Major disputes can take over your life, both professional and domestic, occupying all your waking hours (and many of your sleeping ones as well!).

The Unions will be using 'indicative ballots' to demonstrate the strength of feeling of the membership. They will be setting deadlines and calling for industrial action even though the talks may still be continuing.

The longer it goes on, more distractions will arise and it will be hard not to simply react to every new problem as it arises. You should not allow yourself to lose focus; but this is easier said than done when events outside of the main negotiations are competing for your attention.

Here are just some of the potential problems:

- Insulting comments put on notice boards, emails, websites, etc.
- Violence and intimidation
- Unlawful picketing
- Allegations of management bullying
- Disciplining & dismissal of trade union activists
- Legal proceedings.
- Procedural issues – for example, if it is agreed that no change will be imposed until the procedure is exhausted (sometimes called 'status quo' agreements) what does this mean in practice?
- Internal arguments on the trade union side
- Internal differences on the employers side
- The other side try and go over your head and lobby your constituents

These apparent side issues can easily come to dominate the agenda and distract from the substantive talks to such an extent that one side or the other will insist that talks cannot continue, as a 'matter of principle', until they are resolved. Preconditions and threats of coercion can make progress impossible and protract the dispute. Such things cannot always be ignored, they may have to be dealt with separately, but the priority must be to resolve the dispute and get agreement.

So, no matter how much the relationship deteriorates, informal contacts must be maintained because, without some channel of communication being kept open, talks will remain stalled. One option will be 'talks about talks'. These can focus on process, not the substantive issues, and find ways of restarting negotiations. Acas can often help here and provide a neutral venue for such overtures.

By now you will feel that you are negotiating 'in a bubble', as everything else fades away in importance. The pressures on both negotiating teams intensify as the effects of the dispute start to be felt. Do not be surprised if you start feeling the effects of stress, so watch out for the symptoms in yourself and in others.

One of the causes of this is lengthy meetings. Avoid them if you can and don't set deadlines you don't mean. On the other hand, there will be times when there are no alternative to late nights, and even longer days. Deadlines can be imposed upon you by external factors: the timing of the monthly pay run; the deadline for legally constituted strike action; or, actions necessary to get emergency plans in place which will minimise the impact of the industrial action on customers. If this is the case, be prepared to win what will feel like a war of attrition. Get the comfort factors right, especially for your team.

My longest single meeting lasted over 24 hours. It came at a crucial stage in a rail dispute and it was only one of a sequence of such meetings spread over several weeks. The physical demands on you can be intense – on the occasions I was able to get home, I slept for a few hours and then went back into the negotiations.

Clearly, this is not the best way to make decisions and it is no surprise that mistakes are made and tempers are lost. Nevertheless, there are times when the stakes are high and deadlines are inevitable so there is no option but to keep going until a deal is reached.

Management/Union negotiations differ from most other negotiations in one important respect, doing a deal does not mean that final agreement has been reached; in this context, 'agreement' means that the Union agrees to put management's 'final offer' to a ballot of the membership. Trade Unions are democratic organisations and, whilst, their negotiators will have delegated authority from the membership giving them a mandate for negotiations, they cannot accept an offer on their behalf, indeed to do so could leave them open to legal challenge. These days, therefore, it is rare for a union negotiator to agree unambiguously to a settlement.

The manner in which the Union will put the offer to the workforce is therefore a crucial issue and one that often features in the final stages of the negotiations. The best an employer can ask for is that the union negotiating team will put the offer to the membership with an unequivocal recommendation for acceptance. The union side may well however seek a premium for such a form of words and press for final concessions to achieve this. Conversely, management will seek recommendation as the price of their final offer.

Even where there is agreement to recommend, in some situations management negotiators will remain concerned. If they know that the shop stewards feel that the deal is insufficient, they will suspect that the stewards may be less than enthusiastic in selling the deal to their members. Where trust levels are low managers may believe the stewards will actively campaign for its rejection.

There are weaker forms of words than clear recommendation to accept. A union negotiating team may agree to state that the deal is "the best that can be achieved through negotiations". The meaning of this is deliberately vague; it is a deliberate tactic intended to get the workforce to take the offer seriously, as the alternative is industrial action – in effect 'put up or shut up'.

Finally, union negotiators may only be prepared to put an offer neutrally to the membership, without a recommendation either to accept or reject. Although normally this will not be popular with an employer's side there will be occasions when it is seen as a pragmatic solution to an impasse.

The worst of all worlds is for the final offer to be rejected despite a recommendation for acceptance by the union negotiators. When this happens, the expectations of the workforce will have been further raised. Management's confidence in the ability of the union negotiators to deliver will have been severely weakened and the employer's side are likely to feel that they have already offered virtually everything they can. As a result, subsequent negotiations are likely to become even more protracted and acrimonious. The ongoing relationship between management and union negotiators will have been damaged.

With this in mind, management should show some caution before they disregard union warnings that their offer will not be acceptable to the workforce. Similarly, union negotiators need to be leaders and formers of opinion, and not allow their members to develop unrealistic aspirations.

Sharing information

> *"In war, truth is the first casualty."*
> Aeschylus

Negotiating requires employers to communicate often complex data with trade unions, but this can be difficult to do, especially in a dispute when both sides distrust everything the other side says. Yet this is the very time when you need to share information most of all (despite what some text books might say!) If you do not, the other side will fill the void with information they have produced and, all too often, this will be based on incomplete data, guesses or false assumptions. There is a real risk then that the negotiations will degenerate in to an argument about whose figures are right, with nobody willing to admit that they were wrong.

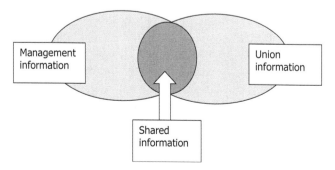

Fig. 5

Management will not be willing to share all they know about a situation (nor should they). After all, 'knowledge is power'. Equally, the trade union will not confide all their knowledge. However, there will be some information that it is in the best interests of all concerned if it is shared.

The parties are unlikely to accept anything that is disclosed at face value and they will want to be able check it for accuracy. The form in which the data is provided needs to allow for this. But, the more this shared information is accepted as non-controversial, the better the chances are that the negotiation will proceed smoothly. Typically, it is management that provide the bulk of this information, as their sources are likely to be superior to those of the union. Nevertheless, the union will be encouraged to share what they know if they can see that there is a genuine sharing of data prior to a negotiation.

Information should be shared between the parties in advance of negotiations for three good reasons:

- Firstly, it is a legal obligation. When a trade union, which is recognised by an employer, requests information under Sections 181 and 182 of the Trade Union and Labour Relations (Consolidation) Act 1992, the employer must provide it if the union would otherwise be materially impeded in their collective bargaining. The Acas Code of Practice 2, 'Disclosure of information to trade unions for collective bargaining' elaborates on this. The Code of Practice not only outlines what the Act says, but it explains what is good practice and gives practical advice on how to disclose information.
- Secondly, because it can simplify and shorten the negotiations by preventing the other side forming their arguments using erroneous data. Disagreements based on different and contradictory information can be the hardest to resolve because they prevents genuine communication. Often the parties themselves do not fully understand how the statistics were derived or on what assumptions they are based. They will however hold to their version of the facts, assuming that the other side is, at best, being economical with the truth and, at worst, deceiving them.

- Thirdly, judiciously used, such data can significantly strengthen your case and weaken the other side's resolve before the negotiations even begin.

Once negotiations are underway, there are a number of tactics that can be employed to manage the exchange of information.

Inevitably, both your presentation and theirs will use statistics to build a case. But, negotiators simplify and use headline indicators, but beware, as always, "the devil is in the detail". There will be some points that you need the other side to understand as they are central to your case. You will need to take these points slowly and use questioning to ensure that they have taken it all in.

Case Study 11

I was involved in a dispute at a print company where the main issue in dispute centred on a technical discussion over the calculation of job timings and bonus pay. The problem was that both sides had produced their own figures and couldn't get them to agree. This disagreement over the facts was threatening to derail the negotiations. As a way of breaking the deadlock I suggested that there be a head-to-head meeting, not of the lead negotiators but of the person from each side who had produced their team's set of figures.

It worked better than I could have hoped. They came back relatively quickly with an agreed analysis. Indeed, this collaborative approach then extended to the main negotiations which were resolved more easily than was expected.

When you are presented with complex data, take time to check their figures and cost any options that are being proposed using these. In particular, be cautious of percentages, they can make the costs seem small but convert them back into actual numbers to make sure. Similarly, watch out for averages, as these can obscure wide variations at the extremes. Always ask to see, and check, the raw data before reaching your own conclusions.

If you need to get into detailed analysis, make sure you have an expert on your team who is able to deal with this aspect of the negotiations. As discussed above, one use of this person is for them to go away with their nominated 'expert' and agree the facts. But don't fall into the trap of thinking experts are independent – they are still advocates. If they bring in an expert, so should you, but there is a danger that it can then becomes a contest of experts talking detail, not a negotiation. Carefully used however, experts can help diffuse tension and resolve deadlocks by focusing on facts, not on positions.

Finally, consider bringing in a trusted third party to produce an independent and impartial factual analysis.

Case Study 12

I did something like this in a dispute over shift patterns at an NHS Trust. Management wanted to introduce 12 hour shifts and were convinced that this is what the nurses wanted. The Union were equally sure that it was opposed by the membership. In conciliation, I suggested that I should facilitate a small group of managers and union reps and draw up a short questionnaire to find out the views of nurses on a ward by ward basis.

This proved successful as it was able to bring out a wide range of views, rather than a simple yes or no vote. Agreement was reached which provided for shift changes but built in support and assistance for those affected.

Unscrupulous negotiators will try and fool you with figures. There is no easy way of dealing with this but, if you are well prepared and take your time to check what you are being told, you shouldn't get caught.

It is also worth considering how to best use case law in negotiations. Employment relations have become increasingly legalistic and now it is both commonplace and prudent for legal advice to be taken as part of the preparation for a negotiation. Unless, however, you are an employment lawyer, or at least very sure of your ground, it is probably best not to exchange examples of case law in support of your case. After all, you may well be seeking a negotiated settlement to avoid having to go to law. If the legal position is central to your case, have a lawyer in your team and get them to speak on this point.

Case Study 13

Many years ago I was conciliating in an employment tribunal case and I thought I could persuade the lawyer representing one of the parties by citing a particularly relevant legal decision. And it worked, at least initially. However, the solicitor got back to me and asked if I had seen a full transcript. I confessed I had not, as I was only working from a summary in a journal. "Well, Mr Hodder" he replied, "if you look at the actual judgement you will see..." and proceeded to demolish my carefully constructed argument.

Not only did I fail to persuade him, I lost credibility but I learned my lesson: don't argue law with lawyers and, if you are a negotiator, negotiate.

Managing the media

"Those who would sup with the devil need a long spoon."
Anon

You cannot negotiate via the media, but you can use the media to put pressure on the other side. You may dismiss such attempts as little more than 'spin', and some employers would rather never speak to the press for fear of being misrepresented. Nevertheless, in these media-dominated days to me it can be a necessity.

In a major dispute, both sides will try to win over public opinion, seize the 'moral high ground' and thereby enhance their bargaining position. So, if you don't, they will and trade unions are getting very adept at putting their side of the story. A war of press notices can be unedifying but if you don't respond, only the other side's story will be publicised. Negotiations are best done in private, but such confidentiality is rarely absolute, so expect leaks to come out and have your defences ready. Whenever I dealt with a major dispute I tried to persuade the parties to restrict what they said to the media and, if possible, limit this to an agreed press notice. In practice, however, this proved very difficult to enforce.

Like it or not, these are features of negotiating in major disputes, so you need to know how to manage the media to get the press onside. Ideally, you want someone experienced in dealing with the media to produce press notices and field their enquiries. And the best advice, when dealing with the media, is to keep your message simple, concentrating on no more than two or three key points.

To this end, you should involve your in-house PR/Communications team right from the outset. They may well already have contacts in the local press that can be of use to you. If you do not have this resource available to you, you might consider buying it in for the duration of the dispute.

Secondly, get your lead negotiator media trained. Your lead spokesperson should look and sound comfortably in front of a camera or on the radio. Someone who is nervous will come over as shifty. You need to maximise your opportunities to put over your key messages and present your side as the innocent party who is doing everything they can to get the dispute ended. Remember, the media give you an unrivalled means of talking to your workforce, customers, suppliers and the general public. It is simply not true that there is no such thing as bad publicity; the attention paid by the media to disputes can be very damaging, so you need to be conscious of the risk to your organisation's image, and defend it.

Internal communications

But, dealing with the media is only part of the task; internal communications must also be a priority. Managers need to be talking direct to the workforce, both with union members and non-members, with employees involved and those not involved in the dispute. Nor should middle and front-line managers be forgotten. All too often, they learn of developments at the same time as their staff and often then through the trade union! Management negotiators need to keep them 'in the loop' as much as possible as they as often leading opinion formers on the shop floor and will be key in delivering any subsequent deal.

The unions may well object, claiming that as representatives of the workforce, all such communication should go through them. But they will be briefing their members and management would be foolish in the extreme to leave such matters to them. In this is a war of emails and notice boards, company negotiators should seek to take control and gain an advantage in a battle for 'hearts and minds'. To do this all internal communications from the company on the dispute should be co-ordinated centrally; it must appear professional in appearance, truthful in content and timely in its circulation.

New channels of communication are being used in employment disputes. The use of social networking sites like YouTube and Twitter, as well as blogs and websites, are all now used to share views, mobilise support and even organise industrial action. Already used in viral marketing campaigns, no doubt employers will increasingly be factoring these into their communication strategies during major disputes. I don't pretend to know how to do this but communication professionals will have a view.

There are always more than two sides to an argument

Workplaces can best be seen as plurality of competing interests. In traditional employee relations, we tend to concentrate on two, management and employees, but this is a gross simplification (albeit one that I have perpetuated in this book by referring repeatedly to 'the other side' in a dispute.) No workforce is homogeneous: skilled workers may well have other concerns than their less skilled colleagues; drivers may well have views that differ from the shop floor; office staff may well see things differently from any of these groups. Equally, management teams can be divided by internal differences and departmental politics. The reality is that many negotiating teams are uneasy alliances of competing interest groups.

Workplaces are necessarily pluralistic and sectional interests are an inevitable part of workplace bargaining. Different groups (departments, locations, shifts, grades, teams, and even individuals) will perceive their interests as being different as well as in common.

In unionised workplace this can mean that more than one union is recognised and negotiating machinery has to be developed to cater for their representation in negotiations. Even where only one union is recognised, it will have representatives drawn from different interest groups.

Some of the most difficult disputes I have been involved in have had this dimension to them. Differences between groups of employees, sometimes but not always represented by different unions, can overshadow proceedings to such an extent that these issues have to be addressed before the substantive issues can be dealt with. Employee representatives need to play a lead role in addressing these internal conflicts, but it is no easy task as such differences can have a long history. Employee reps need to have built a consensus on their side of the table before coming to the negotiations.

Employer negotiators need to understand this role conflict, as it can affect union negotiators' behaviour. Employee reps need to be leaders, but if they go beyond their mandates, if they are too far in advance of their member's views, they will not be able to deliver any agreement they conclude. Reps therefore need to be given the time and the facilities to consult their constituents before, during and after negotiations, if deals reached are to stick and disputes resolved. The involvement of a Union Full-time Officer can be useful here, as they will often bring a wider perspective and give authority and legitimacy to negotiations.

A complication is that certain employee groups have greater bargaining power, by virtue of the market value of their skills, because of higher levels of union membership, greater willingness to take industrial action; or all three factors combined. In such circumstances, management will often have treated them favourably in the past. They will have achieved an established pay lead and enjoy better terms and conditions. They may well be represented by a separate trade union. In such circumstances, which are commonplace in a variety of public and private workplaces, the hostility and sense of grievance between different groups of employees can far exceed any enmity between management and employee representatives. Regrettably, such fundamental issues are rarely tackled – it never seems to be the right time.

Negotiating with more than one union

Sectional interests within a workforce have traditionally resulted in more than one trade union being recognised. However, negotiating with two or more unions separately causes management a problem. From a management perspective, one budget will cover both sets of negotiation, and agreement with one union will affect the size of the pot for the subsequent negotiations with the other unions. Consequently, employers often respond by seeking a common percentage increase across all bargaining units.

As we have already noted, the lead union (typically the largest or the most powerful union) will have more sway with the employer, with the result being that it is this negotiation that will set the going rate. However, the suggestion that one trade union should have its settlement dictated by negotiations with another body will be fiercely resisted, as it will be perceived as calling into question the sovereignty of the other union. Such sensitivities often play on feelings of perceived slights, grade or trade group rivalry, pay differences and even historical animosities. In such situations employers are often accused of playing favourites and buying off the more powerful employees at the expense of the others. Negotiators are well advised to take such matters seriously as they can easily prejudice the prospect of a successful negotiated settlement.

Inter-union hostilities have encouraged the development of "single table bargaining", where unions share seats on the employee side of a joint negotiating body. These seating arrangements can be tricky to set up, and are notoriously difficult to change. Nor do they prevent inter-union disagreements because sensitivities will remain. For example, a union may well resent having negotiations on matters particular to its members being raised at single table forums.

Perhaps the best solution is a hybrid arrangement, whereby an umbrella negotiating body deals with matters affecting all the recognised unions (for example organisation-wide annual pay and conditions negotiations) and meets infrequently. Under this structure, special interest groups meet separately, and more frequently, with management to discuss matters affecting that particular group of employees. There is however no easy answer to such problems and, as a result, they are often left alone. It will be interesting to see if, once the latest round of trade union mergers has bedded down, these problems can be tackled more readily.

Unofficial action

Industrial action can take the form of strikes defined by the Trade Union and Labour Relations (Consolidation) Act 1992 as 'any concerted stoppage of work', which can be for a continuous period (for example, a day, a week, etc.); discontinuous, a number of strikes spread over a period (for example, a day each week for 6 weeks); or, unusually these days, for an open-ended, indefinite period.

Industrial action can also take the form of action short of a strike, for example, 'working to rule' (non-performance of those duties allegedly not specified in employees' contracts); overtime bans, 'non-cooperation' with the employer, or refusing to do certain duties.

By doing this the employees will almost certainly be in breach of their contracts of employment. Furthermore, the union, by calling or endorsing such actions is likely to have induced a breach of contract, an act (technically referred to as a 'tort') which would also normally be unlawful. However, provided the union has complied with the complex rules on notices and ballots set down by statute and called for action in the correct manner, it will have immunity from civil action by those who have suffered loss (employers, customers, etc.). This will then be 'official action'.

Also worth noting is that workers are protected from dismissal for up to 12 weeks after taking official industrial action. Only if the employer can demonstrate that the worker had participated in 'unofficial' action can dismissal take place on these grounds.

However, should a union fail to comply with these detailed legal requirements, the action will be 'unofficial' and the union will potentially be liable for heavy financial penalties. Indeed, should unofficial action be taken by the membership, it must be repudiated by the executive, president or general secretary of the union concerned as soon as reasonably practicable, again in a prescribed manner, if the union is not to be open to civil action. A further potential complication is that, should a legal injunction be obtained to prevent potential unofficial action, and this is ignored, both the union and the individuals concerned could face action for contempt.

The late 1970s saw widespread strikes throughout the private industry and public sector in the UK when on average, 12.9 million working days a year were lost through industrial action, in many cases unofficial and not supported by the trade unions. This increased militancy was attributed by many critics to the increasing importance of 'shop stewards' – employees but also union officials. The 'winter of discontent' of 1978 and 1979 and the subsequent defeat of the Labour Government under James Callaghan saw the rise of Margaret Thatcher. A series of legal reforms which subsequent Conservative administrations brought in severely limited the powers of the trade unions and effectively outlawed unofficial industrial action. Indeed, you might be forgiven for thinking that unofficial strikes are a now a thing of the past.

And yet they can still happen. In February 2009 at the Lindsey oil refinery near Grimsby, hundreds of welders, engineers, pipe-fitters and laggers protested at what they saw as the preferential employment of foreign workers on energy construction projects. Support quickly spread to other sites across the country, no doubt assisted by informal networks of activists and shop stewards communicating by mobile phone. Yet, union officials were not informed or directly involved specifically because, if they were, the unions would face serious financial penalties. Nor should it be assumed that similar problems will not arise in the future.

Such unofficial disputes cause particular problems, not just for unions but also for employers and those who wish to see the resolved. Traditional collective bargaining brings with it structures and procedures for resolving problems. If these cannot be used and union officers excluded, who does the employer engage with to find a solution? Such situations are very uncommon but, should they arise, an employer's first reaction is likely to be to take legal action. I would advocate caution. Taking legal advice is always prudent but suing employees or taking out injunctions against unions may bring short term benefits but the damage done to longer term relationships can be costly. I would suggest that getting talks going immediately on condition that action is suspended is a better position to adopt.

Case Study 14

I was telephoned by a manager of a local transport company who told me that a walk out was being organised at his depot. It would seem that a problem had escalated and frustrations had boiled over. He wanted to know what the legal position was. I managed to persuade him from going to law as the first step.

I immediately contacted the Full-time Officer of the trade union concerned, who knew nothing of the situation as he had not been consulted by the local steward, who admittedly was not very experienced. No doubt concerned to protect his union's funds, he straightaway contacted both the branch and the employer. Action was called off, discussions took place and the matter was resolved.

But, no matter how protracted and acrimonious the dispute, if the organisation is to survive and employees keep their jobs, all disputes must finally be resolved. Nevertheless, the damage done can be long-lasting. I have seen the effects of a national dispute still being felt years later, with worker turned against worker and a lack of trust in the relationship with management. Resentment can continue long after the original causes are forgotten. All of which cannot be good for the viability and profitability of the organisation. There are rarely clear cut winners and losers in major disputes. The best that can be hoped for is a result that all concerned can live with and lessons are learned for the future.

Repairing the damage

"The worst reconciliation is better than the best divorce."
Miguel de Cervantes Saavedra

After the dust has settled, one side needs to take the initiative and start building bridges. There is no point in re-fighting old battles and the two sides will need to do business together again, so it is worth looking to the future. A third-party facilitator can sometimes help in this reconstruction process.

Negotiators can do two things to minimise their chances of again getting into serious dispute:

- Firstly, they can review their formal machinery and ensure robust collective procedures are in place.
- Secondly, can seek to invest in the management/union relationship.

The authors of the Workplace Employment Relations Survey 2004 put this very neatly by saying that procedures provide an "...opportunity to bring consistency to the way employees and employers may raise their concerns, and can equally provide clarity in how situations of possible conflict might be addressed."

Collective procedures

Firstly, negotiators should ensure that the procedures that regulate their interactions are up to date and fit for purpose. These should be jointly reviewed regularly and amended by agreement. Of course, the suggestion that a review should be carried out may cause alarm bells to ring, with union reps in particular suspecting management of having a hidden agenda. It needs to be approached sensitively.

In every workplace where unions are recognised to represent all, or some, employees, proper employee relations machinery should be in place. There should be:

- A **Recognition Agreement** which confirms which sections and/or grades of employees are recognised as being represented by specified union, or unions, for collective bargaining purposes. This has a particular significance in employment legislation: it means that a collective agreement reached with a recognised trade union will vary the individual contract of employment of an employee covered by the recognition agreement, whether they are a member of the union or not. In the UK, collective agreements are not legally enforceable but individual contracts of employment are legally binding.

Acas can provide help drawing up a recognition agreement but, if you want legal advice on a specific point, you should speak to a lawyer specialising in employment matters.

- A **Facilities Agreement** which sets out what will be provided to employees elected or appointed to be union officials to enable them to fulfil their roles in the company. This should specify time off (paid, unpaid and how this will be determined) for trade union duties and activities; use of facilities such as telephones, photocopying, email, the internet, office space and notice boards; plus how they will be able to access to their members.

- Acas has produced a revised **Code of Practice** on time off for trade union activities and duties for consultation. There is also a guide, "Developing effective employee representation: a guide to managing provisions for time off, training and facilities", to accompany the new Code, covering all types of employee representation both union and non-union.

- A **Dispute Procedure** (which perhaps could more accurately be termed an avoidance of disputes procedure) is also sometimes known as a Collective Grievance Procedure or a Negotiating Procedure. There may be subtle nuances of meaning here, but essentially they fulfil the same function. It should provide for two or three internal stages to allow unresolved problems to move to the next level, to be dealt with by more senior representatives on both sides of the table. This 'head room' should allow for the involvement of the Union's Full-time Officer, together with a senior member of management, such as the Managing Director, at the final internal stage. However, the clear and stated intention should be for all issues to be sorted at the lowest level possible. An additional, external stage should allow for the issue to be referred to Acas for conciliation and (by mutual agreement) mediation or arbitration. These terms are explained further in the next chapter.

Other matters that can be specified include: the timings of meetings, who will chair them, who will have a seat at the negotiating table, note taking and agenda setting.

Acas can provide detailed advice and assistance on drawing up and reviewing disputes procedures.

Invest in the relationship

A procedure by itself will not be sufficient. Managers also need to invest in the relationship. It is a regrettable fact that, although most workplaces do not experience repeated disputes, a few undoubtedly do. Whether by accident of history, circumstance or, simply, bad management, these workplaces can have a long tradition of collective conflict and adversarial bargaining. What is worse, relationships between managers and union representatives in such places become characterised by such personal animosity and distrust, that it becomes part of the culture (which I define as "how we do things around here") and is therefore very hard to change. In such situations, even when the parties are not actually 'at war', the best that can be hoped for is an 'armed truce' rather than a genuine cessation of hostilities.

So what can be done? There is no magic bullet, but sustained efforts by management can turn the situation around. As has already been observed, it can take years to build up trust and five minutes to knock it down. Nevertheless, if there is leadership from the top and a commitment to change, it can be done. What is more, if managers can 'walk the walk', as well as 'talking the talk', then union reps may start believing it and respond positively. No one initiative will make the change happen, but a sustained campaign of engagement and communication will. There will, of course, be a cost but not as high as the price you pay for conflict. All the usual rules of change management apply, but there must be a genuine will to change and this has to be communicated to the trade union at a senior level. For it to be believed it must not be seen as a threat, as a sophisticated attempt to marginalise the trade union or as a ruse to subvert traditional bargaining structures to management's advantage.

A good place to start might be for the lead management negotiator to develop a healthy relationship with the Full-time Officer (FTO). To do this, managers need to understand the role of a FTO and how this differs from their own. The two sides of the table are not mirror images: a FTO is not the equivalent of a manager, even if they on occasions look and sound like one. A key difference is that, although a FTO has authority, he or she does not have the hierarchical power of a senior manager. Unions have democratic structures and, however imperfect these may be, a FTO is an employee of the Union and therefore answerable, ultimately, to the membership.

A Full-time Officer is:

- A professional negotiator who can bring with them expertise and a wider experience of the state of the industry.
- Accountable to the membership and will therefore be expected to 'perform' in accordance with the expectations of the local union branch. Relationships with local activists may sometimes be strained, because their expectations can be unreasonable, but FTOs are 'hired guns': they fire the bullets, but the ammunition is supplied by the local reps.
- Accountable to the Union General Secretary and will be required to operate in accordance with Union policy, which generally is set by its national conference. They may therefore be affected by the internal 'politics' of the Union.
- Appointed or elected depending on the rules and structures of the Union. This can influence how a FTO behaves. A management negotiator should make it their business to know if the FTO is facing re-election; if they are, expect more assertive behaviour and 'playing to the gallery'.

In some workplaces, managers welcome the involvement of the Full-time Officer, believing that their wider experience will bring realism to the negotiations and limit unreasonable expectations of the local reps. Elsewhere, managers resist a FTO coming on site, believing that they will better off resolving all matters direct with their local employee reps. Personalities and past history inevitably play a large part in forming these attitudes.

Building a better relationship must be based on mutual respect and both managers and employee reps recognising that they have legitimate and valuable roles to play in the workplace. And the time to start is not when you are in dispute, but when you are not. 'Partnership' may no longer be a fashionable word in some employee relations circles, but a desire to get managers and employee representatives to work together effectively should always be current. Third-party assistance can help with such initiatives, particularly by providing independent facilitation and delivering joint management/employee rep training programmes.

This chapter has focused on major disputes and how to negotiate a way through them. We have looked at some of the problems that can arise and explored ways of preventing such issues arising in future. However, most problems at work do not lead to major employer/ union disputes. Most workplace disputes are far more likely to result in legal than in industrial action. The next chapter looks at a range of options open to managers and employee representatives to resolve workplace disputes both large and small.

10

ALTERNATIVE DISPUTE RESOLUTION

This chapter provides a brief guide to the range of methods that have been developed as an alternative to legal proceedings and industrial action.

If done well, negotiation can be an effective means of resolving disputes in the workplace. But disputes, be they between employers and unions (with threats of industrial action), or between individuals and employers (resulting in employment tribunal claims), still proliferate. So, if negotiation fails, what can be done? All too often the answer is expensive and protracted legal action or industrial action.

Alternative Dispute Resolution (ADR) emerged in the 1980s in America as an alternative to litigation because it was seen as a less costly and time consuming way of resolving business disputes. Originally developed as a means of tackling disagreements over commercial contracts, its application quickly spread to family disputes, neighbourhood disputes, and, of course, employment disputes.

Over the last 20 years ADR has burgeoned, both here and in America, and, despite originally being a means of avoiding going to law, it has been embraced enthusiastically by many lawyers on both sides of the Atlantic and elsewhere. In the UK changes were made to civil procedures rules in 1999 enabling judges to use ADR. Many legal practices now have mediators on their books and there are many reputable organisations in the UK providing mediation services. Some larger, mainly public sector, organisations have set up their own internal mediation schemes. Acas now runs an accredited training course leading to a Certificate in Internal Workplace Mediation for employees who have been selected to be mediators in their places of work.

In fact, Alternative Dispute Resolution in UK workplace disputes has a considerably longer history, dating back as least as far as the end of the 19th century. Acas was set up in 1974 and is by far the UK's largest provider of workplace conflict resolution, for both individual and collective disputes. In this context, Acas services are an alternative not only to legal action but also to coercive action (strikes, management imposition, etc.).

ADR can best be described as a grouping of different, but philosophically related, means of dispute resolution, such as: conciliation, mediation, arbitration, Med-Arb, and neutral evaluation. As a profession, ADR is cursed by internal conflicts over the meaning of these terms, so I hope the following attempts at definition do not prove controversial.

Conciliation & mediation

Conciliation, as practiced by Acas, is where the conciliator brings the parties together to facilitate their discussions. In the collective arena, Acas will typically lead a series of separate and joint meetings of the parties with the aim of helping them reach to reach agreement.

Acas also deals with many thousands of employment tribunal cases each year which could well otherwise result in tribunal hearings. Most of these are dealt with by telephone, as this is the only practical, cost effective way of handling the numbers of such cases. These interventions successfully resolve something like two thirds of employment tribunal applications at great saving both to the taxpayer and the individuals concerned.

Elsewhere mediation has become the preferred term to describe interventions by an independent third-party to resolve disputes. Perhaps in deference to this newer usage, Acas now uses mediation to describe a charged for service they provide for individuals involved in workplace disagreements but who are not pursuing employment tribunal claims.

So why the two terms, conciliation and mediation? In part

the answer is historical. When Acas was set up in 1975 the term commonly used for this activity was conciliation. Since then, no doubt following the American usage, mediation has become the preferred expression used by the growing numbers of private sector providers of workplace conflict resolution services.

Some practitioners say that there is a distinction between the two activities, because mediation must include the making of recommendations and this is not the practice in conciliation. Other mediators prefer a less interventionist, non-directive, counselling approach to dispute resolution. They would argue that their job is to facilitate discussions not to express opinions themselves.

Mediators who see face-to-face meetings and recommendations as central to the process no doubt regard Acas conciliation in employment tribunal claims as a 'watered down' form of mediation. Telephone conciliation has been criticised as little more than message-passing. To me, this underestimates the skills required and challenges faced by these Acas officers who invariably carry caseloads well in excess of anything that could be imagined by other workplace mediators. Message-passing is part of managing the communications between the parties and this need to be done accurately, sensitively and in a timely manner. A conciliator who communicates mainly by telephone has quickly to establish a rapport, demonstrate their independence, demonstrate a command of the subject matter, offer guidance on how tribunals operate, get the parties to reconsider their positions and, yes, pass messages. And they usually have to do all of this without the benefit of a face-to-face meeting!

Personally, I am in neither the directive nor the non-directive camp. When I conciliate I will vary my approach to suit the needs of the situation. If the parties are less experienced or if they have reached an impasse, I will intervene more directly and suggest possible ways forward. Equally, if they are making progress but need a neutral 'referee' to manage the process, I will adopt a more hands-off approach. So am I mediating on some occasions and conciliating on others? No. I believe that both activities are within a range of closely related dispute resolution techniques. For the purposes of this book, I will treat the two terms, mediation and conciliation, as interchangeable.

So how does conciliation work?

This is how I do it. When conciliating in a collective dispute, whenever possible, I like first to talk to the parties by phone and get them to send me any background paperwork (notes of previous meetings, letters, etc.). Often however time pressures prevent this, so I'm quite used to going in cold. Prepared or not, I make a conscious effort not to make assumptions or anticipate what the solution is going to be. A conciliator's job is not to come up with a solution, although I may make suggestions; my job is to create and maintain an environment which allows the parties to do this for themselves. It is their dispute so, if the deal is going to stick, they must have ownership of its resolution.

Conciliation is a flexible process but I like to start proceedings in joint session. After introductions, I explain my role and ask both sides to make a brief statement of the situation as they see it. I then usually split the parties and put them in separate rooms so that I can speak to them privately. It is a judgement call as to whether I speak to management or the trade union team first: usually I start with the one initiating the change that has resulted in the dispute.

My job in these side meetings is to understand the negotiators' concerns and get behind the positions they have adopted. I need to identify the key issues – the deal breakers – as well as points where movement might be possible. I do this as quickly as possible and try hard not to leave one side or the other sitting around waiting for too long as this only adds to the tension.

At this stage I act as a 'Devil's Advocate', with the aim of getting the parties to reassess their stated positions with as much objectivity as possible and consider how they are likely to appear to the other side. Of course, I don't expect everyone to be completely open with me from the outset. I need to gain their confidence by demonstrating my impartiality and credibility; hopefully, as we progress, I will be able to unfreeze their initial positions and get them to look at possible new ways forward.

The next step is shuttle diplomacy. Typically, this involves me in conveying the messages the parties allow me to pass to the other side. I may put these into more neutral language, but I am always very careful to leave the content unchanged. The aim here is to build mutual understanding and explore options on a 'without prejudice' basis. By using me as a channel for communication, ideas can be floated, built upon and, if necessary, withdrawn, without the formality of offers being 'put on the table'.

Needless to say, this can be a time consuming business. I would never encourage late night meetings as a way of brokering agreement because tempers can fray and mistakes made. Nevertheless, if we are working to tight deadlines, late nights can be necessary. If this is the case, the conciliator's job is to keep the parties on track, keep the momentum going, stay positive and keep them fed and watered. One of my first jobs in Acas was to go out and buy late night fish & chips for twenty people!

My aim will always be to get the parties back together again but the timing is crucial. No matter how good my summarising skills may be deals often involve technical matters which must be got right. So, when a breakthrough has been made and we are close to a deal, I always get them back into joint session to confirm where we have got to. This has to be handled carefully as the pressures the parties are under can lead to a breakdown even at this late stage.

My job now is to keep them on task until the details of the deal and its implementation are agreed and written down. Usually there will need to be a ballot of the workforce to confirm the deal and arrangements for this may also need to be included. All of this must be done before the parties and I can go home.

A conciliator has to be prepared to deal with conflict. The pressures on negotiators can be intense and it can be no surprise if the adversarial nature of traditional bargaining sometimes results in negative attitudes and confrontational behaviour. A conciliator has to be able defuse the tension and act as a calming influence thereby allowing the parties to take a step back and re-examine the issues in contention. In my experience, both sides to a dispute may want a resolution but can still find themselves locked into fixed positions which can be destructive both for the organisation and employees' jobs. My job as a conciliator is to free up these positions and help the parties move towards agreement without them losing face. I have often thought that conciliation can simply be defined as getting people off of hooks! And it works. Acas reports that conciliation in collective disputes helps the parties resolve nine out of ten disputes.

Conciliation not only avoids the cost of legal or industrial action, but it can help the parties work collaboratively to develop lasting solutions. A successful conciliation can therefore repair and strengthen relationships. As will become clear in the next chapter, not only do the concepts of mediation, conciliation and facilitation overlap, but they are closely related to, and enhanced by, the 'interest-based', Win-Win Bargaining proposed in the seminal book *Getting to Yes* by Roger Fisher and William Ury in 1983. I shall be looking in more detail at these skills in the next chapter.

Arbitration

Arbitration allows the parties to a dispute to have its outcome determined by the decision of an independent individual (or suitably nominated panel). If the parties cannot agree the resolution of a dispute but need a decision to be made, arbitration may be the answer. An arbitrator, or board of arbitration, can be appointed by agreement between the parties or by statutory provision. Acas maintains a list of suitable individuals for this purpose and will appoint an arbitrator to resolve a collective dispute once the parties have agreed clear terms of reference for the hearing and commit in advance to abiding by the outcome of the process. Unlike commercial arbitration, an Acas arbitrator's decision is not legally binding; it is binding in honour only. Perhaps surprisingly, and certainly encouragingly, this has very rarely proved a problem.

Acas arbitrations are more formal than conciliation albeit not as formal as court of law. The parties are expected to submit written submission of their case to the arbitrator, together with any relevant documents, well in advance of the hearing. These will also be exchanged between the parties. On the day, the parties are asked to present their case; in doing so they can refer to any relevant documents in their submission and call anyone to speak on their behalf. The arbitrator then asks questions of the parties. Usually Acas arbitrations last up to half a day before the arbitrator closes the meeting and notifies the parties of their decision in writing.

It may sound surprising, but I have never been an enthusiast of arbitration. Although far less common than conciliation, I don't deny that it has its place. Over the years, I have been instrumental in getting several disputes I have conciliated in to go to arbitration to the satisfaction of all concerned. However, as a conciliator I would always prefer those in dispute to resolve matters themselves and retain ownership of the resulting deal. My concern is that, by using an arbitrator to make the decision for them, they give up control of the outcome. For this reason, I always make sure that both sides appreciate that, whatever the arbitrator determines, they must be able to live with the decision. As a conciliator, if the parties need to go to arbitration rather than settle matters in direct talks, my task is to get them to agree terms of reference.

This is important because the discretion an arbitrator has to devise an award is determined by the terms of reference. This can be free-ranging, thereby allowing the arbitrator to produce compromise solutions on all the points at issue, or limited within a predefined range. One possibility is to restrict the arbitrator's award to the final position adopted by one or other of the parties in their negotiations prior to coming to arbitration. This latter approach is called final offer arbitration (also sometimes referred to as 'pendulum' or 'flip-flop' arbitration).

Final offer arbitration came into vogue in the 1980s because of its supposed links with 'new style' agreements then being introduced by a few inward-investing Japanese electronics companies like Toshiba and Nissan who were setting up manufacturing plants on green-field sites. These agreements commonly included features like no-strike deals linked to unilateral access to arbitration and sole bargaining rights for a single trade union. Such agreements were also accompanied by what were seen at the time as Human Resource Management innovations: single-status and harmonisation of terms and conditions of employment. However, although these agreements attracted considerable interest amongst commentators at the time, they were never that widespread and few appear to have lasted. Pendulum arbitration in fact predated these agreements and it is still in use, albeit infrequently, as a technique today.

At the time, proponents of this form of arbitration claimed that, if the parties knew they could end up at pendulum arbitration, this prospect would have a calming effect on their negotiations. No one would want their final positions to appear unrealistic because this would reduce their chances of success at any subsequent arbitration. In theory, by thereby moderating their behaviour, the parties would be more likely to reach a deal in direct negotiations, thus reducing the need for arbitration. In my experience this was not the case. I suspect that, in reality, the effect of these arrangements was to encourage negotiators to escalate disputes direct to arbitration as this always held the prospect of a better deal than could be achieved in negotiation.

A further problem with pendulum arbitration is that final offers are usually made up of a list of items, each with its own value/cost. An arbitrator will be required to make a choice between a union's final claim and management's final offer, even when a compromise could resolve the dispute and be less likely to cause problems for the organisation in the future. I've been told that, for this reason, arbitrators prefer not to have their decision-making constrained in this way. It may also be that those advocating final offer arbitration distrust arbitrator discretion, believing that, if allowed to do so, arbitrators will always seek the middle ground and split the difference. All I can say in response is that is certainly not my experience.

Purists would argue that arbitration should not be included in a list of ADR approaches. It is certainly more judicial in its approach than other forms of ADR. Participation in it is voluntary, but it requires the parties to give up any control of its outcome. There is no appeal against an arbitration award, but arbitration has a legal dimension. The 1996 Arbitration Act allows the courts to have a supervisory role, making arbitration proceedings subject to challenge by Judicial Review.

Med-Arb

Med-Arb, as the name suggests, is a two-stage, hybrid process. The parties are invited to explore settlement, with the independent mediator acting as a facilitator/conciliator. If this is unsuccessful, with some or all of the issues remaining unresolved, then the mediator will move into an arbitration mode and make an award. This method of dispute resolution was developed in commercial circles but lends itself readily to workplace disputes.

Somewhat confusingly, Acas has for many years provided what is best termed Collective Mediation. In practice, this is employed when the parties cannot reach agreement through conciliation but, for whatever reason, decline to be bound by arbitrator's award. It is therefore a weaker version of arbitration, with the independent person restricted to making recommendations which the parties, in advance, have committed to giving their serious consideration. For this reason, one Trade Union General Secretary persists in calling it 'non-binding arbitration'.

Neutral evaluation

Finally, a more recent development is neutral evaluation. This concept involves an independent person hearing submissions from the parties, considering the merits of the case and offering a non-binding evaluation of the likely outcome should the matter proceed for a legal ruling or arbitration. It has been suggested that neutral evaluation could be a useful addition to the rules of procedure of Employment Tribunals.

As a process, this has its parallels in the working of the European Court of Justice where Advocates-Generals will give an opinion if the Court considers that a case raises a new point of law. Such opinions may only be advisory and not binding in law, but they are almost always confirmed by subsequent Court judgements.

Although relatively new as a formal judicial process, informal neutral evaluation has always been a part of the tool kit of experienced conciliators. We may not express legal opinions but we can and do point out privately where to the parties' arguments are weak and identify the possible undesirable outcomes of their proposed course of action.

Alternative Dispute Resolution in the UK continues to evolve and its practitioners are now developing their own professional standards and organisation. Managers and employee representatives should be aware of ADR options because, if problems cannot be resolved, the services of a third-party may be the solution.

Additionally, managers and employee representatives could also benefit from acquiring conflict resolution skills themselves. The next chapter explores how some of these Alternative Dispute Resolution techniques can be used by managers and reps in their everyday activities.

11

FACILITATION & MEDIATION SKILLS

This chapter examines how mediation, facilitation and joint problem-solving can help managers and reps resolve conflict in the workplace.

So far the focus of this book has been on negotiation and collective disputes. However, line managers do not often get involved in negotiating terms and conditions of employment. Similarly, employee reps will usually leave such tasks to their Branch Officers. Nevertheless, front line managers and reps are change agents: they play leading roles in managing change in the workplace; they resolve disagreements between individuals, deal with employees with grievances, solve problems and agree ways forward.

Their importance has been underlined by recent changes in legislation. The Employment Act 2009 attempted a sea-change in employment law, with the repeal of the requirement for a three-stage in-house discipline procedure and the encouragement of flexibility and informality to resolve workplace problems at an early stage. But, organisations can put the best procedures in place and still experience unnecessary problems. Managers and reps need to have the confidence and ability to translate these procedures into practice; to achieve this, they need expertise in conflict resolution and, in particular, facilitation and mediation skills.

As will become evident, facilitation has much in common with mediation. In fact, the term 'facilitative mediation' is in common usage in the American ADR literature.

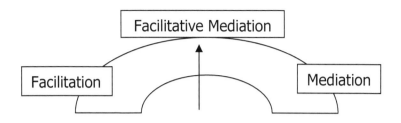

Fig. 6

A dictionary definition of 'facilitation' would be 'the act of making something easier'. In the context of conflict resolution, the term means:

> 'A process whereby an independent person uses their skills and knowledge to assist a group of people work together more effectively and achieve what they need to do. Facilitators make appropriate interventions to manage this process.'

By contrast, mediation is:

> 'a process whereby an independent person uses their skills and knowledge to resolve interpersonal conflicts'. The job of mediator is to encourage a non-adversarial approach to dispute resolution by clarifying misunderstandings, facilitating clear communication, and by getting the parties to focus on the real issues in dispute. A mediator helps the parties develop options by which their dispute can be resolved.'

There is an important distinction between facilitation and mediation: facilitation skills are more likely help a manager or rep help a group of colleagues work together to perform a task or solve a problem; whereas mediation skills are more likely to help a manager or rep resolve disagreements between individuals. The two activities clearly overlap – both can involve conflict resolution as well as problem-solving. But for now, let us keep them separate.

A word of caution, however, although a manager or employee

rep can use facilitation/mediation skills in their daily work, this does not make them a facilitator or a mediator. A fundamental feature of these processes is that this individual is seen as independent by all concerned. Managers and employee reps are not neutral; they are leaders and advocates. The positions they hold give them authority and some power, so they cannot be viewed as independent. Nevertheless, the skills of a facilitator or mediator are readily transferable and well worth acquiring by both managers and employee reps.

Facilitation skills

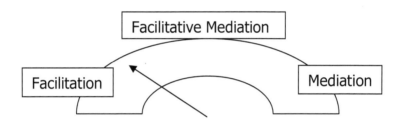

Fig. 7

Facilitation is task orientated. Any facilitator must first establish an objective for the group. This may take the form of terms of reference signed up to by stakeholders or, it can be less formal, with the group itself deciding this for themselves.

Secondly, the facilitator must give thought to the composition of the group: are all the affected groups represented, have any key players been left out? Should there be a better mix of gender, job groups, grades, etc.?

Case Study 15

A few years ago I was asked to develop a new grading structure for an organisation in the not-for-profit sector. At my suggestion, a group was set up of representatives from the main work areas, together with representatives from management. My main contact, and the driving force for the exercise, was the Personnel Manager. I facilitated the group and, after meetings spread over several weeks, a new grading structure was produced which all on the group were signed up to. The scheme was fully equality-proofed and would have resulted in a coherent grading structure for the whole organisation.

It was never implemented. The organisation concerned was very hierarchical and, although responsibility had been delegated to the group, the managers on the group were not Board members and lacked sufficient clout to 'sell' it to the Board. The Personnel Manager was committed to the new scheme, but she was unable to drive it through and as a consequence had to deal with the negative fallout amongst staff because expectations had been raised by the exercise.

Since then I have always insisted on getting a senior manager to sit on any working group I facilitate. In the early stages this can affect the dynamics of group working, but I'd rather have this than have a project fail at implementation stage.

A facilitator's function is then to help this group of people achieve their objective; it is not to lead the group, but to lead the process by which agreement will be reached. The facilitator is a catalyst, there to create the right conditions for progress. Part of the skill is to get the group do the work, not for the facilitator to solve the problem for them. Inevitably, facilitators form their own views on the best way forward but any suggestion made by the facilitator needs to be presented cautiously and the temptation to direct the group to one preferred solution must be resisted.

If the group is to have ownership of the outcome, it must be the group that develops the solution. Input from the facilitator therefore needs to be brief and to the point. The facilitator's role is to keep the group moving forward and make progress through consensus.

When doing this, I found it useful to keep in mind the Tuckman model of group working. Developed by Dr Bruce Tuckman in 1965, it portrays the life cycle of a group from when its members come together to when they disband on completion of the task.

The Tuckman Model of Group Working

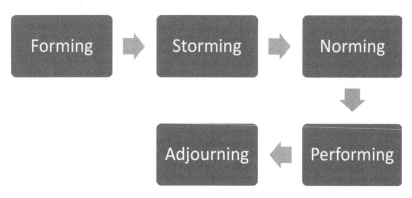

Fig. 8

His four stages: Forming, Storming, Norming, and Performing (he added the fifth stage, Adjourning, later), describe how small groups develop and behave. It can be comforting to know when the group you are facilitating is going through its storming stage, and personal conflicts are coming to the fore that this is normal! But, they will need to get their conflicts out in the open before they calm down, sort out relationships and process issues and start working together productively. Your job is to keep bringing them back to the task in hand.

A facilitator needs to:

- **Be challenging**
  Groups can get complacent. There can develop a false consensus when group members only see things from one perspective and gloss over the potential problems. If this happens facilitators need to be provocative, don't simply tell them the answer but stir them up with a well timed comment. Lob in your grenade, sit back and watch how they deal with it. Groups often need to storm more before they can norm

and perform. Facilitators need to be aware of this and act accordingly.

- **Keep the group focused**

  It is the job of the facilitator to keep the group focused on the task in hand. When they are going off track, the facilitator will need to remind them of their objectives. The group must be forward looking and not allowed to dwell on past failures. However, participants will need to draw upon their past experiences, so the facilitator will need be alert and keep the discussion positive.

- **Stay positive**

  The facilitator must always remain positive and maintain the momentum. When a group gets frustrated with a lack of progress, it is the enthusiasm and energy of the facilitator that will keep them going. It is the responsibility of the facilitator to look and sound upbeat and to inspire confidence in the process.

- **Encourage participation**

  The facilitator must encourage contributions by being welcoming to new ideas and thanking participants for their input. Each group member should feel willing and able to speak and it is the facilitator's job to make sure that they are given an opportunity to do so. To do this the facilitator will need, politely but firmly, to keep in check any excessive talkers and dominant characters. The best way of doing this is to get the group to agree and enforce 'rules for the day' and deal with behaviours that disrupt proceedings. The outcome must be that all participants are listened to and their opinions respected.

  When tensions come to the surface, the facilitator needs to get the individuals concerned to explain the reasons for their attitudes and explore their differences in a honest but non-aggressive manner. By this means, the facilitator must seek to reconcile conflicting views and manage conflict. Bad behaviour cannot be tolerated but emotions, and the reasons for them, need to be explored.

As well as being able to get people to 'open up', a facilitator needs to be able, at times, to 'close them down'. Some group members like to do the talking and, if left unchallenged, can come to dominate the proceedings. However, you need to keep these same individuals on-side as they can have a valuable contribution to make. By contrast, others will appear reluctant to say anything, yet you need to get them involved. Be realistic: you can't change their natures and you have to work with the people you have. The silent type may have good reason for being quiet; the talkative character may be the natural mouthpiece of the group and popular with them.

- **Check progress**
  The facilitator needs to be sensitive to the mood of the group and check how participants are feeling. If the facilitator has concerns these need to voiced and shared with the group in a positive manner. If the group is not content with how it is working, the facilitator can suggest new ways of operating. Equally, it can be helpful to remind the group of how well they are doing and the progress they have made.

Facilitation techniques

Different techniques can help. Silent brainstorming is a useful way of giving everyone equal 'air time'. Each person is asked to think of 3 or more ideas; then you go round the group asking each person in turn for just one contribution and record these on the flip chart. Keep going round until all the ideas have been identified. New options will come out as participants build on previous suggestions. The facilitator acts like a ring master. I make a point of going into the middle of the semi-circle of seated group members. This means I can speak direct to one person and get their views, whilst, at the same time, turning my back on any over-dominant personality to shut them up. That usually works.

Some commentators categorise 'difficult' personalities: the

disruptor, the joker, the know-all, the non-talker, etc., and suggest different strategies for dealing with them. I try and resist the temptation to classify people in this way. I would caution against being over manipulative. You not only risk turning them off, but it is surprising how the group can turn against you if you are seen to be too directive. If you must, speak to the trouble-maker outside of the room during break time, but this should only be done as a last resort.

The facilitator is the expert on the process. It is the facilitator's job to structure the meeting, recommending appropriate techniques to build consensus and generate solutions. An experienced facilitator will have a range of exercises (icebreakers, energisers and brainstorming techniques) that they have used before and feel comfortable with. When acting as facilitator, I always prepare two programmes for the event: an outline one for participants and stakeholders; and a more detailed one for me, which includes approximate session timings and breaks, taking into consideration the techniques I expect to use.

The following are some of the techniques I have used, with varying degrees of success. More information on them is widely available but, ultimately, the only way of learning to use them is to try them out. In the past, I've asked colleagues to be guinea pigs for new exercises I have developed or techniques I wanted to experiment with.

Parking

Ideas and comments come up at inappropriate times. You don't want to lose them and you want to make the contributor feel valued. Have a piece of flip chart paper prominently displayed; write the idea up on it and make sure you return to it at an appropriate time.

Brainstorming

Getting the group to produce new ideas out is central to facilitation. Brainstorming (or, for the more politically correct, 'Thought Showers') is the standard solution. Every time I have used brainstorming techniques, the group has produced more ideas than they could possibly have done as individuals working alone. What is more, with a little practice, they can build on each others' ideas and generate really innovative thinking.

As already mentioned, silent brainstorming has the advantage over normal brainstorming in that it allows everyone an equal opportunity to speak. It can feel less spontaneous and not so interactive, so I usually only employ it early on in a facilitated event. But, as the group gains in confidence, unless there are some very strongly assertive personalities present, open brainstorming can be used without any problems.

Talking walls

This is a refinement of brainstorming and can be used to get more detailed information out in the open, whilst still having the virtues of silent brainstorming. Each person is given one sheet or more of flip chart paper and asked to put up their major concern or preferred option, depending where you are in the process. These are then displayed around the room. Participants are then invited to add their comments on any sheet that they find of interest. The problem here is that it can work too well and you end up with a huge amount of disparate information which can be cumbersome and time consuming to process.

Prioritising

Groups tend to find many issues but have difficult agreeing which are of most importance. The propositions are displayed around the room on separate sheets of flip chart (this technique is often used in conjunction with Talking Walls). The participants are each given three adhesive dots or post-its. These are votes and each person can stick all three on one flip chart sheet or in any combination they choose. The votes are added up to give a ranked list. However, this is a forced consensus and the ranking of ideas is likely to be directly influenced by the composition of the group. Some participants inevitably will be outvoted, so care must be taken to ensure that everyone is signed up to the outcome.

Fishbone and Force Field analysis

Fishbone Analysis, (or Ishikawa, to give it its proper name) became popular as part of the Total Quality Management movement. Used in together with brainstorming, its aim is to map out the causes and effects of a particular problem. The exercise takes the form of a diagram resembling the skeleton of a fish, with four main 'ribs' branching out from the backbone labelled Procedures, People, Policies and Plant (the name of this latter category reflects the manufacturing origins of this technique). The group is asked to analyse each category in more detail by adding smaller bones to each of these and thereby display the whole picture pictorially.

Fishbone analysis

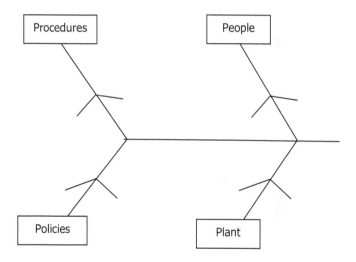

Fig. 9

Force-field analysis is a similar technique used visually to portray opposing forces acting on a situation. Some forces drive a desired change, whilst others restrain it. The strength of these forces can then be given a strength index. By adding up the driving and the restraining forces, it is intended to show the group which forces will prevail. Actions can be identified to limit the restraining forces and build on the driving forces to get the desired outcome.

Force Field analysis

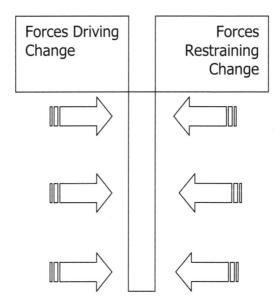

Fig. 10

Personally, I have never found either of these techniques particularly useful. They can easily take too long and, if you are not careful, participants will get lost in unnecessary detail. Nevertheless, they have the advantage of allowing a problem to be depicted visually and I know they are popular with some facilitators.

Pictures and Flow-charts

I find inviting people to draw what they mean very appealing to some group members. Some individuals prefer this way of visualising problems and this technique can free-up their thinking.

Flow-charts are more formal representations of processes. Individuals with project management or computer backgrounds way find this method particularly insightful. I would not necessarily suggest facilitators go as far as using Gant charts, but there could be situations where this might be appropriate.

SWOT analysis

Used together with brainstorming, SWOT is a planning tool which can help analyse the Strengths, Weaknesses, Opportunities, and Threats presented by a project. It can be applied to a wide range of business activities: strategic planning, marketing, product development or even team building. This technique provides a structured way of developing an understanding of what is facing an organisation and can thereby enhance the decision-making process.

My experience however, is that the four categories can overlap, so any facilitator running a SWOT analysis needs to guard against this by explaining that:

- Strengths mean the internal, positive attributes that an organisation has within its control and which can be built on.
- Weaknesses mean the internal, negative attributes an organisation has within its control and which can be addressed.
- Opportunities mean potentially advantageous factors external to the organisation which can be taken advantage of.
- Threats mean external factors, outside of the organisation's control, which pose a risk.

SWOT is not the only planning acronym. There is PEST (Political, Economic, Social, and Technological); which can be extended even further, by adding Environmental and Legal, to give PESTEL.

My own experience as a facilitator of running this type of analysis exercise is mixed. SWOT can eat up all the time available and, whilst it is appropriate for top-level, strategic planning, I have my doubts how good it is for addressing more immediate problems in the workplace. My instinct when selecting a technique is to keep it simple and keep it short. My aim is to get people thinking and talking, and produce practical ways forward. I am less interested in wide-ranging theoretical analysis. With this in mind, I use an abbreviated version which you might call 'SW'. When I get to the option evaluation and selection stage of the joint problem-solving cycle I simply get groups to look at the strengths and weaknesses of a solution. It works for me.

Nominal Group Technique (NGT)

NGT is used to identify problems, generate solutions and prioritise recommendations for implementation. It has been described therefore as a total assessment tool.

There are variations in its operation, but this is the form of NGT I have used. The facilitator opens by stating the question to be addressed (for example, 'how can we reduce absenteeism?'). Silent brainstorming is used to generate ideas, which are collected in the usual 'round robin' fashion, with ideas captured on flip charts. No criticism is allowed and only questions on points of clarification are accepted.

Each group member then votes anonymously, with each having the same number of votes (usually 5 or 6) to allocate as they wish. The results are recorded with the top scoring ideas selected for further discussion. If numbers permit, smaller sub-groups are then used with each one given a different idea to analyse further. These then present back to a plenary session of the full group where the findings of the sub-groups are developed into recommendations for implementation.

NGT combines the benefits of silent brainstorming with the advantages of prioritising solutions by voting. To me, however, it has a number of disadvantages. Firstly, consensus is forced and therefore unduly influenced by the composition of the group. As a result, group members may not feel committed to its outcomes. Secondly, full group discussion is limited and, whilst this can in theory speed up the process, it curtails creativity and the development of genuinely new ideas. Thirdly, in practice I have found it a time consuming and rather tedious process. In my experience, it is unsuited to working with large groups because the voting process is too laborious. The problem here is that the facilitator is supposed to get the group to vote on all the ideas that they have generated, yet these will be numerous, especially when working with more than a handful of participants. What is missing is a 'clumping' of ideas to reduce the number of alternatives to manageable proportions. For these reasons, I no longer use NGT in this form. I prefer a joint problem-solving cycle approach.

The problem-solving cycle

The task of the facilitator is to guide a group through a process of joint problem-solving. There are various problem-solving cycles, but I use a simple, five-stage approach.

Fig. 11

Stage 1

The starting point is the task the group has been given. The group need to be reminded by the facilitator what they are there to achieve. It may be that everyone knows each other, so formal introductions may not be necessary, but even then group members need to know why each person is there. The facilitator should explain the joint problem-solving process and get the group to agree how they will work together. A good way of doing this is to get agreement on rules of behaviour for the day, and display these prominently on flip charts. I usually do this by splitting the group into two and asking one subgroup to brainstorm positive behaviours for group working ('what will make this group well?') and the other group to look at negative group working behaviours ('what would make this group work badly?'). This gives them some practice in brainstorming and gets them talking. The rules they develop should include: no interrupting a group member, no personal criticisms, mobile phones to be turned off and confidentiality (although, in practice, this is difficult to enforce).

The facilitator needs to make sure that the necessary arrangements have been made: seating in the room should be laid out in a semi-circular fashion, without any tables to act as barriers; there will need to be a plentiful supply of flip chart paper; and, refreshments made available. Facilitation is not a quick fix, so sufficient time and resources must be allowed (I usually insist on a full day being set aside as a minimum). Off-site meetings can be helpful to prevent interruptions and give the event sufficient status.

Stage 2
The group then should be encouraged to explore the problem, with each participant describing it from their own perspective. Initially, the discussion is unstructured but the facilitator must ensure that no one is attacked or criticised for seeing the situation as they do. If the problem is complex, brainstorming can be used to identify the different strands that will need to be addressed. This stage is brought to a close by the facilitator who summarises the discussion and reframes the problem in a manner in which all can sign up to.

Stage 3
The next step is option generation. A standard rule agreed at stage 1 is that group members must not attack the views of others. But time must be given for debate as participants must be allowed to challenge ideas they do not like. A good way of doing this is to use an option generation technique during which criticism of the contributions of others is not permitted. When working with a group for the first time I prefer to use the 'silent' brainstorming techniques referred to above. The facilitator should stress that there are no 'bad' ideas and demonstrate this by encouraging group members to build upon the ideas of others. The facilitator then 'clumps' these into broader

categories (this can be done by consensus, but I have found that this often takes too long, so I usually do it when the group are having a break). I then ensure the group agrees to the categorisation I have produced and make any amendments as requested.

Stage 4

The group then debate the 'clumped' options to determine which ones should be adopted. The final selection is a particularly key stage. Sometimes groups of options can be aggregated further to produce an agreed way forward relatively easily. On other occasions the debate may require longer to achieve consensus. One way of achieving this is for the facilitator to get the group to produce agreed criteria (e.g. budget, impact on staff morale, time, etc.) and to make these criteria as tightly defined as possible. On other occasions the facilitator will use consensus forcing techniques (prioritising, ranking, etc.) but care needs to be taken with this approach as you can only progress with the agreement of the group. Try too hard to force the pace too quickly and you will lose consensus.

Stage 5

The final stage is action planning. The group need to be encouraged to stay on task and put their agreed options into an implementation plan with timings and action owners (who, what, when and where). At the end of the exercise a report must be produced to record the work of the group. This can be written by the facilitator or by a nominated group member. In theory, if progress has been recorded openly on flip charts as the group went along, then the report writing should be non-contentious. But, if there is any possibility that this might not be the case, the facilitator should take responsibility for the task.

In most cases when I worked as a facilitator I volunteered to write up a final report which described the process and set out the agreed action plan. In doing so, I used the flip charts which had captured progress at every stage of the process and, where possible, copied these verbatim. I then cleared the report in draft version with group members. The group need show that they were all committed to the recommendations of the report and a good way of doing this is to get them to make a presentation to the commissioning parties – often this is the senior management team, the Board or, where a union is recognised, to a joint meeting of management and union officers.

It could be argued that there are two further stages of the facilitation process: Implementation and Review. As an external facilitator I was only rarely involved in implementation, as this was the responsibility of the parties. Indeed, for me to be so could interfere with their ownership of the outcomes of the exercise. I did however make it a practice of building into the action plan a formal review of outcomes and implementation, usually 12 months into the future, and indicate that I would be available to facilitate this if needed.

Problems with facilitation

Facilitation is not a quick fix because, by progressing only by consensus, you move at the pace of the slowest, most doubting group member. But remember, having this person on the inside of the group is better than them being on the outside, where their opposition will damage the prospects of the group's work being implemented. You need to get the doubter on-side. When you succeed in doing this, they will become your strongest ally and you will need them when it comes to selling the group's conclusions to stakeholders.

Don't forget, a facilitator's job is not to change a doubter's views about everything, only just their view on how to solve this particular problem. Often it is the most reluctant person who has the most to offer, and they may only be saying what others are thinking. As ever, don't be afraid of conflict, get curious and explore what the real reasons are for opposing the ideas under discussion. The facilitator's job is to take the group forward, step by step, reaching agreeing each stage. By this method, when the final solution emerges, the doubter won't oppose it.

As already identified, managers can have particular difficulties being facilitators. After all, managers are paid to manage aren't they? For managers, facilitation means:

- Giving up control over the outcome and empowering the group.
- Not having a direct input into decision-making and maximising

the input of the group.
- Not leading the group but leading the process.

So, you need to ask, is facilitation the right approach to tackle the issue in hand? Have you the time to facilitate – if there are real time pressures, perhaps an instruction would be better? Has facilitation already been tried but consensus proved impossible? Is facilitation ducking the issue – are you trying to avoid responsibility? Have you the authority to change existing arrangements? Have you the training, skills and, most importantly, commitment, to follow this approach? Would the independence and experience of an external facilitator be more appropriate?

Facilitation is not a panacea for all the problems of the workplace but, by involving employees, using their knowledge and experience and getting their buy-in, it can result in solutions that are not only better, but more likely to be successfully implemented.

Mediation skills

Fig. 12

Mediation and facilitation are closely related but, if facilitation is about problem-solving, with mediation the focus is on a non-adversarial approach to dispute resolution. Mediation certainly works. A colleague of mine mediated in a case where the two individuals in an office had not spoken to each other for many months. One can only imagine the fallout from this for the company. Mediation got them talking and put their relationship back on track.

Managers deal with conflicts of interest, be they formal grievances or informal complaints, disciplinary issues or low level performance issues. For many frontline managers, this is their day job. As already noted, managers cannot be a mediators, (at least not in their own work areas) because they are not seen as independent. How can they be? They are too involved and, if they are not, they should be! But managers can use mediation skills to deal with disputes between individuals in the workplace.

Part of the problem is power and how the manager is perceived by the individuals concerned. Managers have situational power flowing directly from their role in the organisation (although of course newly-promoted managers can feel uncomfortable when faced by an assertive employee or experienced representative). But when going to mediation, all concerned must enter the process feeling that they will be treated as equals. Indeed, it is the job of a mediator to ensure this is the case. But, the workplace is far from egalitarian. Aside from status associated with their relative position in a hierarchy, individuals may feel disadvantaged because of their lack of seniority, length of service, job security (temporary or permanent contracts), or communication skills. Nor should we forget the possibility that the individuals might feel that they have been discriminated against because of the race, gender, sexual orientation, disability, religion or belief, trade union membership (or non-membership), social background, or any combination of such factors. This point will be returned to later.

An external mediator can go some way to remedy the implicit power imbalance in a situation. They start then with an advantage because they come from outside and can therefore be seen as independent (although the issue of who pays the mediator will need to be discussed and agreed). Large organisations can have their own panel of internal mediators drawn from volunteers amongst their own staff. They need to be carefully, selected, trained, supported, and attention needs to be paid to which cases they are allocated, but these problems can be overcome. However, this will not suit smaller organisations, nor will in-house mediation always be appropriate in highly sensitive cases.

A mediator will be aware that how they conduct themselves must, at all times, reinforce this perception of independence. After all, the parties are being asked to put their trust, and possibly their future, in the hands of an unknown person. It is the job of the mediator to quickly build trust and demonstrate their integrity. In encouraging them to engage in mediation, the mediator will explain the process, discuss their concerns and explore the alternatives.

Secondly, mediators bring with them their own power by virtue of their role. They must exercise this by challenging any inappropriate or discriminatory behaviour. It requires them walking a fine line: the parties must be helped to deal with the past but not dwell on it and, instead, look to the future. They must not be allowed to blame all their problems on the other party but they must feel that they have been allowed to have their say. Mediators need also to attend to any special needs the parties may have and call for breaks to diffuse tension and allow the parties to gather their composure. Finally, the mediator is responsible for the pace of the meeting; too slow and the parties will become disheartened at the lack of progress. The mediator must give off enthusiasm and positivity, because these emotions are infectious and are needed to maintain momentum. The mediator needs to build consensus, because the process can only move by agreement and there can be no shortcuts to achieving this.

Individuals will have reservations about coming to mediation and it is part of the mediator's task to encourage them to do so but without pressurising them. Mediation is voluntary and it takes those on both sides of an argument to agree to the process. Its appeal can be that it gives the person involved a chance to express their feelings and be protected from any animosity this might provoke. The mediator therefore provides a 'safe environment' where the issues can be explored. It requires the commitment of the parties to participate: to speak, listen and try and work things out.

Can a manager adopt a similar approach? In one respect a manager has an advantage; they are at least a known quantity. Trust is clearly the first hurdle and much may depend on what has gone before and the manager's existing reputation. But exactly what is the manager proposing? This needs to be made clear. A manager can offer to arrange talks between the two individuals, without any preconditions other than their agreement to take part, and without prejudice to any other steps the individuals may take subsequently. The manager can chair the meeting and seek to use mediation techniques in an attempt to resolve matters amicably. But the manager could be placed in a difficult position. Supposing in the discussion matters are revealed that should result in disciplinary action? There are no easy answers to this dilemma because it comes back to a manager's role in the organisation.

Let's look then at a typical mediation by an independent third-party, and assess which of the skills and techniques are readily transferable. Different mediators, and different organisation delivering mediation services, will have their own style and working methods. I use the same facilitation problem-solving cycle but with the emphasis on dispute resolution.

Fig. 13

Stage 1

Having gained the agreement of the parties to come to mediation, the Mediator will hold separate meetings with the parties. At these, Mediator will explain the mediation process, describe the role of mediator and impress on the parties the importance of confidentiality. At this early stage the motivation of the mediator must be to start building a rapport with the parties, demonstrate impartiality and gain their trust.

The Mediator uses private discussions with each of the individuals to find out more about the situation from their perspective and to begin to explore their initial aspirations. To do this the Mediator will need to recognise and acknowledge the parties' feelings.

In these side meetings, the Mediator will confirm the parties' willingness and commitment to continue with the mediation process. This stage allows the Mediator to prepare for the mediation and plan a strategy for taking it forward. Included at this planning stage will be the arrangements for a suitable, neutral venue for the mediation.

Stage 2

The Mediator will welcome the parties and explain that the purpose of this part of the process will be to clarify the issues between them. The Mediator will then set the ground rules, stressing, in particular, the confidentiality of the process. It is sensible again to remind the parties of the process they are in. A key feature of this stage is to provide each party with an uninterrupted opportunity to have their say. It is likely that this will stimulate some conflict and the Mediator will need to manage this

The Mediator will now summarise the situation and reflect this back to the parties, getting their acknowledgement that this is a fair description of the situation. The accuracy of this summary will be crucial. It must cover all the major issues, fairly reflecting the views of the parties. It must not avoid sensitive or emotive issues but, where possible, should reframe these by putting a positive emphasis on what is achievable. As well as covering what is in dispute the summary should include areas on which they agree. The Mediator will then agree an agenda that will tackle the issues identified.

Stage 3

This stage will generally be run in joint session, although the Mediator may call for side meetings to allow the Mediator to explore the issues in more depth with the parties. The aim will be to get behind the issues, address concerns and identify the interests that will need to be satisfied to reach a resolution.

Throughout the Mediator will encourage honest and open communication and check back with the parties to avoid any misunderstandings. To do this, the Mediator will summarise and reflect back to the parties, highlighting both their areas of agreement and of disagreement. By acknowledging differences it will be possible to move on and start changing their focus, from the past to the future. The Mediator's role is to manage the process, remaining positive, reminding the parties of the progress they are making and bringing them back to the agenda. It will also require the Mediator to be flexible and get the parties to agree changes to the agenda should this prove necessary.

As the stage progresses, the Mediator will encourage the parties to start developing ideas as to how the dispute can be resolved. These options should emerge naturally from discussions and, as they do, the Mediator will record them and thank the parties for their efforts.

Stage 4

The Mediator will highlight the ideas and suggestions that have come out of the discussions. At this stage the Mediator will encourage the parties to assess these as options by adopting a joint problem-solving approach. The aim at this stage is to start putting together agreed ways of resolving the dispute. In doing this, the Mediator will continue to note and thank the parties for their conciliatory gestures.

Stage 5

The Mediator will confirm with the parties what they have agreed. The Mediator will then produce a written record of the agreement, action planning the steps that now to be taken for this to be implemented, including any actions for follow-up and review. The action planning must be practical, recognise what the parties have achieved and any objectives included in it should be as SMART (Specific, Measurable, Attainable, Realistic and Time-based) as possible. The agreement must dispose of the issues that were in contention and be future-focused. The confidentiality of the agreement, or any part of it, must be directly addressed. As with the resolution of any collective dispute I have been involved in, the parties should sign the agreement to record their unambiguous commitment to the actions contained in it.

Where agreement has not proved possible, the Mediator will identify with the parties their possible next steps. The Mediator will close the session, noting that this marks the end of the process, remind them of the need for confidentiality and thank the parties for their hard work.

Mediation skills for managers

So, can managers use mediation skills in the course of their work? Yes, but as will be evident from the above, the demands on mediators are considerable.

A mediator needs to be able to demonstrate at all times their integrity and be able to build and sustain a rapport with the parties. Specific skills include: positive listening, questioning, diplomacy, the ability to give accurate feedback and summarise to check understanding and buy-in. A mediator must have well developed people skills: they need drive, patience and be able to focus on the future whilst dealing with the detail of the present. They must be able to demonstrate warmth, show respect for the views of others, have empathy and be organised but flexible when managing the agenda and chairing meetings. Finally, central to the work of a mediator are conflict resolution and consensus-building skills.

Mediation therefore requires a wide range of abilities, but it is interesting to note that almost all of these are also needed to be an effective negotiator and, for this reason, have already been identified and explored in some detail in earlier chapters. But there is one additional demand on facilitators and mediators, and this is neutrality. And, as with facilitation, the fact that they are not seen as neutral can prevent mangers from being mediators in their own workplaces. Mediators and negotiators may share many common skills, but negotiators, be they managers or employee reps, are by their very nature partial.

So, as was noted at the outset, although a manager may not be able to be independent, with these skills and attributes, they may be able to adopt a mediation approach to inter-personal conflicts in the workplace.

But, despite the utility of mediation skills, some mangers will feel themselves unable to approach a problem with this mindset. After all, managers are paid for their judgement, so they may well feel uncomfortable being non-judgemental. Managers are leaders, and thus more accustomed to leading discussions than facilitating them. They may even feel incapable of abandoning their habit of telling people what to do. Yet this is what adopting a mediation approach to inter-personal conflict will require of them.

Even when a manager, or indeed an employee rep, is able and willing to take a mediation-style approach to workplace issues, there will be occasions when it is inappropriate.

Such occasions will include where there may have been a serious breach of workplace rules, for example allegations of assault, discrimination or harassment. Managers and reps should be aware of the agreed procedures for dealing with such matters which, after investigation, could lead to dismissal or even prosecution. In such cases procedures need to be followed, indeed an attempt to use mediation could be regarded as avoiding or trivialising serious misconduct.

In less serious matters, a mediation-style approach may still feel inappropriate because the manager (or employee rep) feels too personally involved or perhaps the attitudes of the parties to a dispute seem too entrenched. There are a number of reputable organisations that provide trained and experienced mediators for just these situations, for example: the Centre for Effective Dispute Resolution (CEDR); Total Conflict Management (TCM); Workplace Mediation UK; and Acas.

Another approach to dispute resolution is for organisations to have their own employees trained as in-house mediators. Again, a number of organisations deliver such training and support. Acas delivers training towards a Certificate in Internal Workplace Mediation, which is accredited by OCR. Candidates are assessed through their performance in role play activity on the course and by presentation of a portfolio of evidence after one month the course is completed.

I would suggest that all employers should give some thought to how mediation could be used in their workplaces and discuss with their employee representatives how this could best fit with existing procedures and suit their particular needs. A good place to start is to compare their existing discipline and grievance procedures with the principles set out in the revised Acas Code of Practice No. 1, Disciplinary and Grievance Procedures which Employment Tribunals will take into account when making their awards. Also worth considering is the new Acas guide on Discipline and Grievances at Work. Although this does not carry with it the authority of the Code of Practice is does contain practical advice on how to handle discipline and grievance cases. Both documents make explicit reference to the use of mediation, particularly at the informal stages of procedures and especially where there has been a breakdown in working relationships.

12

OTHER PERSPECTIVES

"Experience without theory is blind, but theory without experience is mere intellectual play."
Immanuel Kant

This chapter looks at three theories which give a psychological, a mathematical and a sociological perspective on workplace negotiation.

So far we have concentrated almost exclusively on the practice of dispute resolution. This next chapter is given over to three distinct theoretical approaches selected for the sole reason that they resonate, albeit in different ways, with my own experiences.

I am, however, not a psychologist, a mathematician, nor a sociologist. I am only a practitioner in the dark arts of collective bargaining. So, if my lack of expertise in these fields has resulted in any inaccuracies and oversimplifications, I apologise. My aim has simply been to provide summaries which might whet the appetite and suggest to other practitioners who find themselves similarly interested where further study might prove rewarding.

Transactional analysis
Transactional Analysis (commonly known as TA) was developed by the Canadian-born, San Francisco-based, psychiatrist Eric Berne in the late 1950s. Berne came from a Freudian background but moved away from traditional psychoanalysis to produce his own theories of social

psychology based on people's interactions. TA seeks to understand human behaviour by looking at what he called the 'transactions' that occur when people interact.

Transactional analysis attained popularity with the publication of Berne's first book, *Games People Play* (1964). But the real best seller was *I'm OK, You're OK* (1964) written by Berne's friend, Thomas Anthony Harris, which became one of the most successful self-help books ever to be published. Although his book popularised TA, it was dismissed at the time by many mental health professionals and traditional psychoanalysts. Its critics have called it pseudo-science. But, although now less popular than it once was, it has subsequently been taken up by many marriage and family counsellors, and used by educationalists as well as by management and organisational development consultants. It is a world-wide movement, with the Institute of Transactional Analysis in the UK, the European Association for Transactional Analysis and the International Transactional Analysis Association.

But has it relevance for negotiators? At one level, transactional analysis is a theory of communication. Berne used the term 'transactions' to describe the flow of interactions between people. It is this focus on communication, and how their transactions reflect the participant's mental states, that can be of interest to negotiators. The following is intended only as a brief introduction which cannot therefore do justice either to the complexity of transactional analysis or its development as a discipline since Berne's day.

Berne postulated that each of us has three "ego states": Parent, Adult, and Child, which he believed were directly influenced by our childhood experiences. Each of these states comes with associated feelings which underpin particular behaviours, vocabulary, gestures and body language.

The Parent

The Parent ego state is a set of feelings, values, attitudes, thinking, and behaviour that were conditioned into us by our parents and affected by events during our early childhood. The Parent state comes in two forms: critical and sympathetic. In communication it is revealed through angry or impatient body-language. In this mode we can sound judgemental, critical and patronising.

The Child

The Child ego state is a set of feelings, emotions and behaviours which we access from our childhood. Irrational by nature, the Child in us can prompt positive or negative feeling about ourselves and dictate our reaction to external events. In communication it can come over in laughter or in anger. It is displayed in child-like behaviour: tantrums, giggling, whinging, exaggerated language and gestures. But the child state should not be seen as necessarily negative; it can also express itself in charm and creativity. The Child state comes in two forms: Adapted (which is reflected in compliant or withdrawing behaviour) or Natural (which is seen in spontaneity, creativity and rebellion).

The Adult

This ego state gives us our ability to think, evaluate data, make rational decisions and objectively appraise of the world around us. The Adult in us keeps our Parent and Child in balance. In communication it comes over in confident, positive, non-threatening behaviour. It is displayed by rational discussions, reasoned argument, and attentiveness as well as by asking questions.

For Berne, successful communication between two people requires their ego states to be complementary. Complementary transactions are Parent/Child (or Child/Parent), Child/Child and Adult/Adult.

So if the person initiating the interaction is in a Parent ego stare, and the person receiving the interaction responds in a Child state, the transaction will be complementary. This will provoke a further response, again with a complementary transaction, and a chain of such interactions will follow.

Returning to negotiation, what might this look like?

My interpretation is that, in Transactional Analysis terms, traditional bargaining can often be Parent/Child. Whilst this will be a complementary transaction, if the Child responds in a Natural manner (i.e. rebelliously), the relationship is likely to be adversarial. Equally, if the Child acts in an Adapted manner (i.e. is withdrawn), progress will be difficult. Diagrammatically, it would look like:

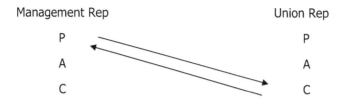

Fig. 14

The dialogue could go something like: Management "what you are seeking is not acceptable"; Union "that's typical of you...."

By contrast, Win-Win Bargaining is Adult/Adult., and would look like:

Fig. 15

The dialogue might sound like: Management "why don't we discuss ways of making this possible?" Union "OK, what are your concerns?"

But, if the transactions are not complementary (for example, Child/Adult) then, according to Berne, the transaction will be crossed and will remain so until one or both of the parties to the interaction change their ego state so that a complimentary interaction can take place. If this does not happen, and neither gives way, communication is frustrated, leading to anger and frustration.

In a negotiating setting it might look like this:

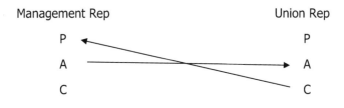

Fig. 16

For example, Management open from an Adult ego state perspective, saying: "3% is the average level of settlement in the industry this year." The Union responds from a Child state saying "I don't care about that, 3% is pathetic."

The transaction is crossed, so there is an ineffective communication. The situation can only be rescued by a reciprocal, complementary transaction. So, if management shift their state to Parent and respond by talking about values (e.g. fairness) then negotiation can get underway. Alternatively, they could persist in Adult mode and see if the other side shift to Adult to match them. If neither happens, there will be a communication breakdown

Interestingly, Berne identified that some individuals often try and pressurise others (or be pressurised themselves) to match their preferred communication style. So, an employer negotiator who persistently negotiates from a Parent ego state is likely to provoke a negative Child-like response in the Union side. What is worse, if the other side does not comply, and responds from a different ego state, they will be regarded as trouble-makers!

Berne went on to look at where a series of complementary interactions leads to: he described the possible outcomes as procedures, rituals, pastimes and games. In TA, a procedure is a simple series of complementary, adult transactions developed for a purpose (for example, how to drive a car). A ritual is similar in that it is also a simple series of complementary transactions, but rituals are set by external social forces and conventions. These can be quite informal (how we behave when we meet someone) or formalised (like a religious ceremony). As we have already seen, collective bargaining has its own particular rituals.

Pastimes seem rather innocuous. Like games, they are a series of transactions that are reciprocal and semi-ritualistic but, unlike games, they are forms of small-talk which serve as time-structuring activities to ease social intercourse. Games are of far greater concern for the adherents of TA. In *Games People Play*, Berne defined a game is *"an ongoing series of complementary ulterior transactions progressing to a well-defined, predictable outcome"*. These games are not fun to play! They are the dysfunctional, devious and "toxic" ways that people seek to achieve "strokes" – Berne's term for a unit of human contact and recognition. He identified dozens of such games and claimed that more were always being discovered. He gave them such catchy titles as "If it weren't for you"; "Let's pull a fast one on Joey"; "Look what you made me do"; and, my favourite, "Now I've got you, you son of a bitch!"

Berne made great claims for these games, which he saw as being played by *"innocent people engaged in duplex transactions of which they are not fully aware, and which form the most important aspect of social life all over the world."* I am not aware of Transactional Analysis having identified games played by negotiators, but it would be an interesting area for further research. Would, for example, the behaviours I have labelled 'Dirty Tricks' be regarded by TA practitioners as negotiator games?

So what, for me, are the lessons that negotiators can draw from Transactional Analysis? I am attracted to it as it could provide a possible explanation of the outbreaks of childish behaviours which I have seen on both sides of the negotiating table. I am intrigued by the idea that traditional bargaining is often locked into Parent/Child ego states. And, as a conciliator, I am interested in the idea that my real task is to guide people into Adult/Adult transactions. Certainly it seems to me that, for integrative bargaining and joint problem-solving to be successful, it needs to be conducted openly as an interaction between Adults.

Game theory

Game theory is a branch of applied mathematics which seeks to model the interactions of agents who act out of self interest and adopt strategies to optimise the benefits that will flow to them. In this respect it makes many of the assumptions used in classical economics. The development of Game theory owes much to the mathematician John Forbes Nash, who has been the subject of several books and the biopic film, *A Beautiful Mind.*

Nash was notorious – aggressive, utterly self-confident to the point of arrogance, and highly eccentric. He was eventually committed to hospital for paranoia. He was, however, a mathematical genius, who built on the earlier work by John von Neumann to develop Game theory.

In 1950 Nash received his doctorate from Princeton and joined the RAND Corporation, the American top secret Cold War think-tank. His work was to apply Game theory to military and diplomatic strategy against a background of the real possibility of a nuclear war. It has been claimed that Game theory contributed to the understanding of how a policy of nuclear deterrence could work which, in turn, led to arms control talks. Those post-war years are perhaps best summed up by the acronym, MAD – mutually assured destruction.

Four years later, Nash had to leave RAND because of his unorthodox behaviour, and went back to pure mathematics, where he continued to produce ground-breaking insights, particularly into the understanding of the geometry of objects in higher dimensions and the solution of nonlinear partial differential equations.

By the 1980s, the impact of his early work in Game theory had spread beyond mathematics to philosophy, economics, evolutionary biology, computer science, political theory, and, more recently, artificial intelligence and cybernetics. In 1994 Nash, recovered from schizophrenia, he shared the Nobel Prize in Economic Science for his work on Game theory. He is again working on Game theory.

So what can Game theory tell us about workplace negotiation? John Nash realised that social interactions were rarely zero-sum, because they combined competition and co-operation. Perhaps he helped the Cold War warriors of the RAND Corporation realise that nuclear warfare could never be win-lose, it had to be lose-lose.

Despite its apparent successes, Games theory is not without its critics who regard its assumptions as unrealistic. As any practitioner knows, negotiators do not always act in a completely rational manner (a fact recognised in Transactional Analysis). They do not have a perfect knowledge of the options available nor do negotiators necessarily even know exactly what they want. Rather, the perceptions of the parties affect their behaviour and their preferences. They react to the behaviour and language of their colleagues and of their opponents. How they feel, their values and personal ambitions, together with group dynamics and inter-personal relationships, all impact and shape negotiator behaviour.

Secondly, few negotiations are between two autonomous individuals; normally they are between negotiators, or teams of negotiators, who are answerable to their constituents that shape their mandates and influence the bargaining process, albeit indirectly.

Games theory, therefore, (like Homo Economicus of economic theory) give an oversimplified and idealised pictured of negotiators as perfectly rational beings who make informed decisions to further their self-interest. Real people, and their motivations, are far more complex and dynamic.

But does this matter if Games theory accurately predicts human behaviour? Game theory certainly comes to some interesting conclusions which might be of help to workplace negotiators. The story starts with Nash's solution to the Prisoners' Dilemma Game. In 1951 he produced his equilibrium solution where both players get a worse outcome than they could have achieved had they co-operated.

The Prisoners' Dilemma Game tells the story of two prisoners (Prisoner A and Prisoner B) who were accomplices to a crime. They make a pact not betray one another and not confess to the crime. They are put in separate cells and accused of a crime, but the police lack enough evidence to get a conviction unless one, or both, confesses.

The prisoners have two options: confess or not to confess. This is sometimes called defect (from their agreement) or co-operate with each other (by not confessing). If neither of them confesses, then both will be convicted of a lesser offence and sentenced to 1 month in prison. If both confess, they will get 6 months each. However, if only one of them confesses, and turns Queen's evidence, he will be allowed to go free and his testimony will convict the other prisoner who will get 9 months in jail.

For the 'Dilemma' to work we have to assume that the two prisoners only concern is to minimise their own prison sentences, caring nothing for the fate of the other.

The matrix below sets this out this situation diagrammatically:

	Prisoner A does not confess	Prisoner A confesses
Prisoner B does not confess	-1 / -1 months	-9 / 0 months
Prisoner B confesses	0 / -9 month	-6 / -6 months

Fig. 17

The best option for both prisoners would be not to confess; that way they would both only get one month in gaol apiece – that would be their 'optimal' solution.

But, both think "Supposing I don't confess, but he does, I will get 9 months in prison, which is the worst possible outcome for me." The best answer then to whatever the other one does is to confess. So, both confess and both get 6 months in prison. This is the Nash equilibrium solution of the game which, by definition, is 'sub-optimal'. The two rational, self-interested players end up worse off than they could have done by trusting each other not to confess.

In "win-lose" terminology the table looks like this:

	Prisoner A does not confess	Prisoner A confesses
Prisoner B does not confess	WIN / WIN	LOSE / WIN
Prisoner B confesses	WIN / LOSE	LOSE / LOSE

Fig. 18

But this is a one-off transaction. Workplace negotiations are rarely like that: negotiators will have done business together in the past and will do so again in the future. The Prisoner's Dilemma can be played repeatedly so that the parties build up a history of their interactions and learn from them. (I'm not sure how this fits in with the story of their imprisonment.) This version of the game is known as the Iterated Prisoner's Dilemma, and is therefore closer to negotiation reality.

In 1959, another Nobel Prize winner, Robert Aumann, claimed that rational players, playing endlessly, could achieve the WIN-WIN, optimal equilibrium. This finding was reinforced in 1979 when Robert Axelrod of the University of Michigan hosted a tournament to see what kinds of strategies would perform best over an extended period of playing the Iterated Prisoner's Dilemma. Somewhat surprisingly, it was found that the most aggressive, cheating strategies were less successful than strategies with a capacity for forgiveness and cooperation.

From this it was concluded than the evolution of altruism, in nature and in games playing, could be explained by the pursuit of self interest. Thus, even distrustful antagonists could logically come to co-operate.

I recently came across a quote attributed to Rabbi Hillel, a first century BCE Jewish religious leader, who rather neatly summed this up:

> "Selfishness beats altruism within groups. Altruistic groups beat selfish groups. Everything else is commentary."

This statement was used to explain the latest thinking on Darwinian natural selection operating at the level of groups of animals. Thus, it is claimed, groups of animals (and therefore, by inference, societies of people) that cooperate in an altruistic, co-operative manner will thrive at the expense of groups that act solely in a competitive manner.

Axelrod seems to have come to a similar conclusion. He analysed the most successful strategies and came to some interesting conclusions. He found that, based purely on self-interest, the best strategies involve:

- Not 'defecting' before the opponent does;
- Always retaliating;
- But, after retaliating, co-operating again;
- Not striving to score more than the opponent.

So, despite its simplistic and unrealistic assumptions, does Game theory have a message for workplace negotiators? To me it seems to demonstrate that, provided a negotiator remains trustworthy, a balance of coercion and co-operation will be the best policy. For negotiators then, a synthesis of the coercive/adversarial and the gain-sharing/Win-Win approaches to bargaining is likely to be in the best interests of both parties.

Dramaturgical theory

The American sociologist Erving Goffman developed the idea of dramaturgical theory in which he argued that peoples' actions derive their meaning by reference to their context – their time and place – and how they are seen by their audience. He saw social interaction as drama, with people assuming already existing roles. This performance can take the form of ceremony and ritual in everyday life. For Goffman, a person's very identity and idea of 'self' is determined as they take part in the activities of everyday life. Consciously or unconsciously, they adopt various personas in ways similar to how an actor plays a new character.

Raymond Friedman applies this perspective to examine workplace negotiations. His book *Front Stage, Back Stage: The dramatic structure of Labour Negotiations* provides an alternative to the rational-actor model of Game theory. He uses the metaphor of theatre to explain the continuing appeal of traditional negotiation to its participants. He sees it as persisting because the rituals of negotiating satisfy the well-established expectations of its participants.

I find this approach particularly revealing because it provides a perspective on the impact of audiences and constituencies on the complex dynamics of workplace negotiations. It therefore gives a fuller picture than that provided by psychologists who tend to concentrate on the interactions of negotiators in one-to-one contexts. Their focus on such things as perception and cognitive bias are interesting, but lacks the wider dimension of groups and constituents. Certainly the approach adopted by Friedman describes the reality of workplace negotiation better than any other theory that I have come across.

For Friedman, therefore, negotiation is theatre. Participants adopt roles and, as they perform their parts, they interact with an audience made up of opponents, their own side and constituents. Indeed, I would suggest this audience is potentially even wider; the public, politicians, customers, suppliers, can all be interested parties who, to a greater or lesser extent, seek to influence the negotiators. These onlookers have pre-existing expectations of negotiators based on past encounters and stereotypes as to how negotiators should behave. Such behaviours become formalised into established practices and become the rituals of collective bargaining. So, the two sides sit facing each other across the negotiating table because that it how it is done.

Negotiators are 'actors' giving a performance. They play roles and fulfil the role expectations of others. Their performance is evaluated both by the other side and by their own side. Thus these members of the audience are also participants, who impact on the outcome of the drama. Lead negotiators must show, by their performance and how they deliver their lines, their loyalty and commitment to the cause. Their team members and constituents will expect it.

The negotiating table is the 'front stage' where the parties engage formally in negotiations by acting out the roles of adversaries, representatives and opponents in front of an audience.

For Friedman, breaks in the negotiations allow negotiators to withdraw 'back stage' where they can relax and step out of character. I disagree slightly: in my experience, the action continues back stage, with team meetings, private meetings with constituents, 'corridor' meetings, and caucus meetings. Far from relaxing, negotiators take on different roles, as they engage with their team members and key constituents in what has been called 'intra-organisational bargaining'. Working as a conciliator required me to move between the front and back stage of disputes and this is where the difficult work was done. 'Back stage' is where lead negotiators must take the lead and act as opinion formers and facilitators, seeking to reach consensus amongst their own team members and the factional interest groups they can represent. Before going any further they must get their side to commit to any new tactics, agree what concessions can now be made and, if necessary, change their mandate. To use Friedman's language, they must try and 'write the script' for the next scene.

According to Friedman, this 'front stage' / 'back stage' divide allows for private understanding and public conflict. It is certainly true that the 'theatre' of negotiation allows negotiators to 'play to the gallery' and take up positions that go down well with their constituents. Indeed such things may need to be seen to be done. To get resolution, however, the negotiations need to move beyond such positioning; good negotiators are able to use signalling to indicate possible areas of movement and make informal contacts (often 'behind the scenes') to reach private understandings that can become the basis for formal agreements.

Friedman makes a point that I can certainly sign up to: he states that *"Negotiators can do negotiations in a way that is somewhat more integrative and more like traditional sidebar meetings between lead negotiators [i.e. 'corridor' meetings], but they usually cannot (and would not want to) drop all expressions of conflict or use only integrative tactics."* As he goes on to say, negotiators are under considerable role pressures and constituent expectations to stay in their traditional roles. He seems therefore to conclude, albeit reluctantly, that any attempt to transform labour negotiations is likely to be overwhelmed by the social logic that created these traditional rituals in the first place. I find his realism refreshing.

To me the dramaturgical interpretation adopted by Friedman provides a description of workplace negotiation that most closely accords with my experiences. Similarly, I find his rather downbeat conclusions all the more sensible for their modesty. I agree with him that there is room for traditional negotiators to adopt integrative negotiating practices without abandoning the collective bargaining rituals that continue to serve a useful purpose for them and their constituents.

Certainly my reading of Game theory and Dramaturgical theory lends support to my belief in the possibility and desirability of a synthesis of traditional and integrative bargaining practices. Transactional Analysis gives an indication as to how this merger of techniques could be achieved. Negotiation should be an Adult/ Adult discourse. However, the psychological pressures on us can lead to the excesses of Parent/Child interactions, with patronising and overbearing behaviour going hand-in-hand with childish outbursts. If we can identify it and understand it, perhaps we can deal with it in a more effective manner.

13

CONCLUSION

Managers and employee representatives will always have to deal with conflict because change affects individuals and groups differently. Some will have fears and concerns, so for them change will appear threatening and need to be resisted. For others it will be seen as presenting opportunities. Inevitably then there will be differences of interest (and this simple fact should be recognised and accepted) but, equally, there will also be many areas of common interest. The challenge must be to manage these conflicts and build on the common ground. Conflict may be inevitable but, handled well, it can be constructive and healthy because it will allow the organisation, and the individuals in it, to adapt to new situations.

In this book we have looked at different ways of resolving workplace disputes and we have found that these approaches can be complementary. But when should one method be used rather than another? When is traditional negotiating appropriate? When should less adversarial, Win-Win bargaining or joint-problem-solving be used?

There are no easy answers because it will depend on the history and culture of the organisation; whether a trade union is recognised, the expectations of those involved and the level of trust that exists between them managers and employee representatives.

I have found that the issue affects whether resolution can be reached through an adversarial or a win-win approach. As a general rule, it is easier to have negotiations over pay (which is bargaining on the allocation of scarce resources), even if the outcome is perceived as 'win-lose'. By contrast, joint-problem-solving lends itself to situations where innovation and creativity are required (for example over changes to working practices). However, this is only where trust levels are sufficiently high to make this style of joint working possible.

In fact, pay talks often embrace a number of non-pay matters. It can be useful therefore to take these 'off the table' and deal with them aside from the negotiations. Thus an item calling for action to tackle equality and diversity issues could be the subject of a management/ union working group using joint problem-solving techniques, possibly employing an independent facilitator. This would allow the parties to continue to negotiate in a traditional manner, without the adversarial nature of the pay talks spilling over and preventing collaboration on other matters of common interest.

It is also possible that an issue can initially be dealt with through negotiation, be moved into joint-problem-solving mode only to return to traditional bargaining. For example, where an employer is seeking to introduce productivity related pay, in the first instance this could be an item in the annual pay and conditions negotiations. By mutual agreement, this could be referred to a joint problem-solving working group, perhaps assisted by an external facilitator, to design a new bonus scheme. Such a group would be made up of individuals selected by management and the union not to act as their delegates but chosen because of their knowledge and experience. They would be allowed to work privately, without interference and given facilities and time needed to undertake their task. Having completed its work, the group would then present its report to the joint negotiating body. Having accepted the scheme in principle, this body might well then return to negotiations to agree new pay rates. Over time, it is possible that confidence in such an alternative approach, and trust in the relationship, might grow sufficiently to allow a joint problem-solving approach to be used more widely.

It should not therefore be assumed that the two forms of bargaining are mutually exclusive. Over the years I dealt extensively with rail companies. Working with a colleague, I ran numerous negotiation training events for managers and trade union representatives. At these we talked about both traditional collective and Win-Win bargaining. And, although the rail industry is seen as a bastion of adversarial negotiation, it was suggested to me by union reps that they do use a form of Win-Win. At depot level there is need for agreement on driver rosters which conform to various rules around rest days, consecutive days worked, etc. As anyone who has ever been involved in the subject will know, drawing up rotas is highly complicated and specialised business. I was surprised to learn that, at one depot at least, these were agreed at local level by a form of option generation with the results then compared to pre-agreed standards. It sounded a lot like Win-Win bargaining to me.

So, if management want to expand the use of a non-adversarial, problem-solving approach to resolving disputes in their organisation, what should they do? Changing the rules of the game is not easy.

Case Study 16

I was called in to conciliate in a dispute where the company's new American owners had decided to adopt a win-win approach to the annual pay talks. After years of traditional negotiating with the union, with offer and counter-offer, final offer and final, final offer, this year was to be different. The Managing Director stood up and gave a presentation. He stressed that nothing was ruled out or ruled in and that they wanted to work jointly with the Union to develop options, agree standards and achieve a win-win agreement. His new management team then got up, one-by-one, and each gave a PowerPoint presentation explaining both the finances of the company and the win-win approach. Finally, it was the Union's opportunity to speak. The Full-time Officer got up, looked at the MD and said "so what's your offer?"

Management didn't know how to respond. The company wanted to play by different rules, but they hadn't first gained the agreement of the employee representatives. The result was suspicion on both sides, with management forced to abandon the attempt and return to conventional, adversarial negotiation. A settlement was eventually reached in conciliation, but not without some severely strained relationships.

Far more planning would have been needed for the change of approach described in this case study to have had any prospect of being successful. In these circumstances, union negotiators will naturally be suspicious and their concerns would need to be addressed up front before any attempt could be made to resolve the pay talks. Without extensive preparatory work, it would be no surprise if the union saw it as little more than a strategy by management to sideline the trade union or even as a forerunner of derecognition. I would also suggest that starting with the annual pay round was over-ambitious. It would have been better to use a less controversial subject in the first instance. Success breeds success, so what was needed was experience of previous positive outcomes to build up mutual confidence in the process.

In this book we have also looked at Alternative Dispute Resolution and considered how some of these practices can be used in the workplace. Most day-to-day problems managers and employee reps encounter are minor disagreements (between individuals or teams) or instances of poor performance and behaviour. If left unattended, such matters can become formal grievances or disciplinary issues but, nipped in the bud, most can be resolved without the need for formal action. To assist with such problems we have looked at mediation skills and facilitation techniques.

Much then can be done to tackle conflict in the workplace. Organisations should review and reform their existing procedures and up-skill their managers in dispute resolution techniques. But also, I believe there is a need for joint training of managers and employee representatives in negotiating best practice. My experience is that this will not only improve their abilities as negotiators but, by investing in the relationship, it will build trust, resolve conflict and establish a genuine dialogue between managers and employee representatives.

Steve Hodder
HODDERconsulting

APPENDIX

SO, ARE YOU A GOOD OR BAD NEGOTIATOR?

The following analysis is not based on any scientific study. But, having conciliated in innumerable disputes, and been able to watch managers and employee representatives drawn from a wide range of backgrounds in action, the following are my conclusions.

I hope these statements neatly sum up much of the good practice discussed in this book. Some of these descriptors are simply opposites: a 'good' negotiator is a good communicator; a 'bad' negotiator is a bad communicator. But others are more subtle: a good negotiator is sceptical, whereas a bad communicator is cynical or, perhaps even worse, naive.

You might like to go through this list and assess yourself. Looking back at how you have performed in the past, where do you think you are on a range between each of these statements?

A GOOD NEGOTIATOR WILL:		A BAD NEGOTIATOR WILL:
+5 ⟵———————	0	———————⟶ -5
Be trustworthy, act with integrity	⟵——⟶	Be unreliable, dishonest
Be a good communicator	⟵——⟶	Be a bad communicator
Be emotionally intelligent	⟵——⟶	Be unable to cope with emotions in self or others
Be capable of making decisions (and make the right ones!)	⟵——⟶	Avoid making decisions (or make the wrong ones!)
Stick to mandate	⟵——⟶	Exceed their authority

Be courteous & show respect	⟷	Be arrogant, patronising & rude
Keep the bigger picture in mind	⟷	Get lost in the detail
Show self confidence	⟷	Be egotistic
Show a sense of humour	⟷	Appear humourless or act the comedian
Be practical	⟷	Be over-theoretical
Be inventive	⟷	Be unimaginative
Be mentally tough	⟷	Give in under pressure
Be thick skinned	⟷	Be over-sensitive
Be persistent & focused	⟷	Be easily distracted
Be unafraid to face an issue head on	⟷	Back down easily
Be sceptical	⟷	Be cynical (or naive)
Appear likeable, but not afraid to be unpopular	⟷	Seem ingratiating, seek popularity
Be a good actor	⟷	Be transparent
Be able to admit to mistakes	⟷	Try to cover up errors

Fig. 19

How did you do? You may well know how you should act, but do you always do it when the pressure is on? Are there areas where you know you could improve?

I have run a great many training sessions on negotiating for both for managers and reps and, with a little prompting, most of them would seem to know, in theory at least, what it takes to be a good negotiator. But knowing what you should do is not enough; it takes training and practice to be a good negotiator.

I also believe that, to gain these skills, you need to be able to review and evaluate your own performance, perhaps with a colleague on whose views and confidence you can rely. This can be through a formal mentoring relationship or by informal 'buddying', but support and constructive input from a trusted source can be invaluable.

If you are already an experienced negotiator, you may not feel the need to reflect a great deal on what you do. Usually you will know instinctively what is the right course of action however testing the situation maybe. If asked why you pursued a particular line of questioning or decided to use one tactic rather than another, you may be hard put to say why you did it, but just because you may be unreflective doesn't mean you are not effective.

The 'Conscious Competence' learning model developed by Gordon Training International has, as its highest level, unconscious competence. Here the skill that has been learned has become so practised that it enters the unconscious parts of the brain and becomes 'second nature'. Top sportspeople are like this; they train long and hard so that, when they need to, they can react in a split second, even before their conscious brain has a chance to respond.

Negotiators should indeed aim for this level of performance because, with it, and in the heat of a negotiation, you will trust to your instincts and know what to do. You may not why you do something, but you will 'know' it is the right thing to do.

However, there is, I believe, a further level to aspire to – I call it 'Out of Body Negotiation'. This is where, with practice and experience, you are not only able to watch others but, at the same time, watch yourself as you perform. From this perspective, you can you can assess all aspects of your own performance and the effectiveness of the tactics you are using; you can even listen to yourself speaking.

If you can achieve this, and it is possible to do, you will be able vary your approach and respond immediately with confidence to developments in the negotiations as they unfold.

You will be at the very top of your game.

BIBLIOGRAPHY

Accompaniment and representation in workplace discipline and grievance, prepared by Richard Saundry, Valerie Antcliff and Carol Jones (University of Central Lancashire) on behalf of Acas Research and Evaluation Section, 2008.

The Art of Negotiation, Gordon Wade Rule, 1962 http://www.wifcon.com/pubs/artofnegotiation.htm

Bargaining for Results, John Winkler, Pan Books, 1982

Developing Effective Negotiation Skills, Richard Graham, Huthwaite Research Group Limited

Front Stage, Back Stage: The Dramatic Structure of Labour Negotiations, Raymond Friedman, MIT Press, 1994

Games People Play, Eric Berne MD, Penguin Books, 1968

Getting Past No, William Ury, Random House, 1991

Getting to Yes: Negotiating Agreement Without Giving In, Roger Fisher and William Ury, New York: Penguin Books, 1983

How to Negotiate Better Deals (4th ed), Jeremy Thorn, Management Books 2000, 2009

Managing Conflict At Work, Imogen Haslam and Ben Willmott, CIPD Employee Relations adviser, 2004.

Managing Difficult Conversations at Work, Sue Clark and Mel Myers, Management Books 2000, 2007

Negotiate the Best Deal, Gerald Atkinson, Director Books, 1993

Negotiation Skills in the Workplace, Larry Cairns, Pluto Press, 1996

Negotiation Skills, Baden Eunson, John Wiley & Sons, 1994

Negotiation Skills and Strategies, Alan Fowler, CIPD, 1996

Negotiating Tactics Made Easy, Lawpack, 1999

The Power of a Positive No, William Ury, Hodder & Stoughton, 2007

Practical Negotiating in 90 Minutes, Stephen Morse, Management Books 2000, 2005

Prisoner's Dilemma, William Poundstone, Doubleday, 1992

Successful Negotiating, Patrick Forsyth, howtobooks, 2002

www.salesskills.co.uk/pdf/whitepapers/NEGS-developing_effective_negotiation_skills.pdf

INDEX